"In this fascinating parable, Dr. Mumford provides the key elements to transforming your organization and building a winning culture."

Patrick Manak

Senior Executive Vice President
The National Association of Collegiate Directors of Athletics (NACDA)

"Great leaders amalgamate their life experiences and apply them in a way that enables them to extract the best out of individuals and teams. They also learn how to eradicate behaviors that can be demotivating for teams and businesses. In **INVEST!**, we follow two great leaders and how they apply the lessons of leadership to make their teams and companies successful. Dr. Mumford provides an excellent framework for readers to use as they pursue leadership models that deliver results."

Deirdre Drake

Executive Vice President/Chief Human Resources Officer
U.S. Cellular

"As a thirty-four-year YMCA professional, I recognize the challenges and rewards that good leadership may provide. Dr. Mumford has provided you an opportunity to INVEST in your leadership capacity.

This is a must-read for all leaders and aspiring leaders. You won't be disappointed. Happy reading!"

Paul L. Stoney

President and CEO

YMCA of Greater Charleston

"Dr. Mumford had me drawn in from the start. This is a must-read for anyone leading a team, full of important information and valuable takeaways. When utilized, the lessons shared here are sure to take your organization to the next level."

Annie Sanders

President/CEO

United Way of Gratiot and Isabella Counties

"I strongly recommend **INVEST!** for leaders at all levels and organizations. Dr. Mumford provides great insight on the types of motivation needed to create an exceptional culture that will lead to outstanding results for any organization."

Mark L. Steele

Superintendent

Indian River School District

"INVEST! *is a great book for any leader looking to inspire employees to unheard-of heights of creativity, collaboration, customer satisfaction, and bottom-line financial success. It does an excellent job of communicating, in an easy-to-understand format, how to deal with the critical challenges facing most organizations.*"

George E. Kikano, MD

Vice President for Health Affairs/Dean, College of Medicine
Central Michigan University

"*Dr. Vince Mumford has hit on a winning recipe for leadership development and personal growth. This book is full of time-tested principles that will help leaders, teams, and organizations move forward faster!*"

Bishop Travis Hall

Life Church International

"*Dr. Mumford gets it right. Most organizations don't suffer from a lack of talented people; mediocre results generally stem from a leader's inability to set the vision, inspire, and, most importantly, create engagement throughout the organization.*"

Malisa L. Bryant

Senior Vice President of Contract Sales
Herman Miller

"Dr. Mumford skillfully takes readers on an exciting journey demonstrating the important role an inclusive and effective culture plays in advancing lasting organizational change."

Andreason Brown

Chief Financial Officer and Treasurer

The Spencer Foundation

"Dr. Mumford's creative use of the parabolic style brings his readers into contact with relatable characters and principles that can transform their organization. He makes learning painless and interesting by cleverly weaving important business principles into a fiction story line that keeps the reader engaged to the end."

Pastor Gene Haymaker

Senior Pastor

Maranatha Baptist Church

*"I have been simply amazed by the work Dr. Mumford has done for years and witnessed firsthand how he uses powerful leadership principles to inspire engagement that transforms people and organizations and helps them to perform better. **INVEST!** is perfectly suited for communicating those powerful leadership principles that are critical to the success on an organization. I recommend this book as an important tool for anyone who wants to become a better leader and make a difference in their organization!"*

Stan Shingles

Assistant Vice President

Central Michigan University

HOW GREAT LEADERS **ACCELERATE SUCCESS** AND **IMPROVE RESULTS**

INVEST!

DR. VINCE MUMFORD

Advantage.

Published by Advantage, Charleston, South Carolina.
Member of Advantage Media Group.

ADVANTAGE is a registered trademark, and the Advantage colophon is a trademark of Advantage Media Group, Inc.

Printed in the United States of America.

10 9 8 7 6 5 4 3 2 1

ISBN: 978-1-64225-136-4
LCCN: 2019912866

Book design by Wesley Strickland.

This publication is designed to provide accurate and authoritative information in regard to the subject matter covered. It is sold with the understanding that the publisher is not engaged in rendering legal, accounting, or other professional services. If legal advice or other expert assistance is required, the services of a competent professional person should be sought.

This book is dedicated to Vest, one of the greatest ambassadors of the pay-it-forward philosophy. Vest has used his gifts to make the world a better place by helping so many young people achieve their dreams.

It is my hope that this book continues Vest's legacy of making a difference in the lives of others by inspiring a new generation dedicated to making a difference in the world by paying it forward.

CONTENTS

HALFTIME

Q3

Q4

POSTGAME

FOREWORD

There is an abundance of leadership books on the market, all containing various approaches to successfully managing organizations. *INVEST! How Great Leaders Accelerate Success and Improve Results* is different. It addresses the importance of leading, not managing, organizations through performance development, selecting the right team, and creating an environment where internal and external customer service is superior. These approaches move an organization from managing to leading and accelerating success through direct and intentional investment in the organization's real bottom line: people!

To paraphrase the opening of Charles Dickens's novel *A Tale of Two Cities*, these are the best of times and these are the worst of times; yet, this is a time when leadership is critically important. Now is also the time for leaders to invest the best of themselves in those they are entrusted to lead and encourage these actions to be replicated. In other words, pay it forward, a clear lesson gleamed from *INVEST!*

This investment in others also requires us to care, which I have operationalized as the demonstration of Compassion, Appreciation, Respect, and Empowerment. This profoundly humanistic approach will move organizations forward and result in the jettisoning of outdated beliefs on leadership. Moreover, as made clear in *INVEST!*, leadership is also a calling to serve each other. This service can and should take a variety of forms; and one of the most important forms, as demonstrated in this significant work, is kindness.

Dr. Mumford, a writer and scholar whom I have known for many years, knows of what he writes. *INVEST!* provides clear and thoughtful strategies for accelerating the performance of organizations to achieve impressive outcomes through the use of engaged and thoughtful leadership. This wise and relatable narrative allows the reader to immerse himself or herself in a complex series of challenges through the eyes of the protagonist, Ray, and unravel important lessons that enable him to turn a troubled organization around while igniting organizational energy and transforming the workplace.

I believe you will find *INVEST! How Great Leaders Accelerate Success and Improve Results* worth your investment. It is fun and engaging, but also practical and effective if applied. Its four-step program will enable you to create innovative and accountable work environments where teams are empowered to make a difference by using their talents and gifts to support the organization's overall growth, development, and impact.

Make these the best of times, by investing!

Alicia B. Harvey-Smith, PhD
President
Pittsburgh Technical College

PROLOGUE:
LOST

ONCE UPON A TIME ...
TWENTY YEARS AGO

It was raining hard, in painful, unrelenting sheets of water through nonstop lightning and terrifyingly loud thunder. It had been this way for hours, and the storm had seemingly worsened ever since he left the bus station and began walking to the university. The lightning strikes seemed only a few feet away, as did the thunder, right overhead.

His appointment with the dean of admissions had been earlier that day. He had missed it. The bus delivered him hours late, due to the storm. It was his first trip this far from home and was supposed to have been a day trip. He had no arrangement for a place to sleep that night. For lack of anything else to do, he continued to walk toward the university. He hoped that he would find someone there.

He had never in his life been so wet or felt so alone. As he made his way to the admissions office door, he drew in his breath and knocked, hard. He looked around for a doorbell, and, not seeing one, he knocked again, harder. He didn't think that anyone would be able to hear his knocking over the sounds of the storm. The door stayed shut, and the windows of the office were dark. He looked around.

There was a single source of bright light that shone among the dim streetlamps that dotted the campus path. He walked toward it, recognizing the university's sports stadium. If the lights were on there, he thought, possibly there would also be an open door. He could get out from under the rain. Hopefully his clothes would be dry by morning. Then he would be able to explain to the admissions office about the bus being delayed. He hoped that they would understand. He hoped that when he hadn't shown up for his appointment, the scholarship he was there to discuss hadn't already been given to someone else.

He walked into the stadium and saw a man standing inside the door. The man looked up; he had a friendly face.

"Hello," the man said, extending his hand. "Are you lost?" he asked the exhausted young man, as they shook hands.

Shivering, the young man politely explained about the delayed bus and missed meeting with the dean of admissions, that when he went by the admissions office, no one had responded to his knocking.

"Yes, it's after hours now. That office has been closed for a while," the man said.

The young man let his shoulders slump. He felt defeated. He was unsure what to do next. He tried to gather his thoughts.

The man looked at him with concern and said, "Hey now, don't worry. We'll fix this. My name is Vest."

Vest led the young man to a seat in his office, stopping on the way to hand him a handful of towels to dry off. A warm drink was prepared and drunk. Vest called the dean of admissions at home. He explained what had happened and confirmed that the dean would be free to meet the next morning.

Vest took the young man into the stadium apparel store to pick out some university gear, pointing out the items that the athletes at the college wore. The young man changed into the dry clothes. Vest showed him the team's industrial clothes dryer, which, he promised, would have the young man's own clothes warm and dry in record time. He added with a warm smile that the university team gear items were the young man's to keep.

As he changed into his new, dry clothes, he heard Vest make another phone call and give his name, but he couldn't imagine to whom. He saw that the offices in the stadium had couches in them. Now that he was warm and dry, he thought he might be able to sleep there in comfort and wake up in time for his appointment with the dean. He felt relieved and grateful to have met Vest.

Vest walked back into the office. He carried a bag with the newly dried clothes. He said that the dean of admissions had confirmed he would be available to meet at 10:00 a.m. That would leave plenty of time for the young man to make the 2:00 p.m. bus, which would take him back home.

Vest said, "You've got a place to sleep—let's get you there."

The young man tried to explain that he hadn't booked a place to sleep and had no more money. He asked if he could stay on the couch in the office until the next morning. Vest repeated himself, then added that it had all been taken care of. The young man felt overwhelmed and gratefully followed Vest out to the car. When they arrived at a nearby hotel, he thanked Vest, over and over, for driving him there, for drying his clothes, for getting him new clothes, and for calling the dean.

"You can thank me by having a good meeting tomorrow with the dean," Vest said.

The young man promised he would.

THE NEXT MORNING

At the meeting with the dean of admissions, the young man began by nervously apologizing for missing the previous day's meeting. He then thanked the dean for the gift of the night in the hotel.

The dean looked up, surprised. Then he said, "Those thanks belong to Vest. He paid for your hotel room, is my guess. The school certainly didn't. That's typical of Vest. He's an incredible person, isn't he?"

The young man agreed, wholeheartedly. Then he wondered about an envelope he had found that morning, in the bag of dried clothes that Vest had handed him. He hadn't opened it yet.

The dean had good news: the young man would be admitted to the university on a full scholarship. He added that scholarship students who wanted to work while attending the school were allowed to do so as long as they kept up their GPA. In fact, the dean said, many students worked for Vest's sport organization.

The young man was delighted to hear that. He left the admissions building wearing a huge smile and jogged to the stadium to find Vest.

On his way to the stadium, he took the time to open up the envelope from Vest. He was touched—but at this point not surprised—to find a printout of a new, paid-for bus ticket back home, as well as some cash for snacks.

He was still holding the ticket and cash from the envelope when he found Vest at the stadium. All the young man could say, over and over again, was thank you. Thank you. Thank you. He remembered to ask if he could work for Vest once the school year started. Vest laughed, cautioned him about the importance of maintaining a good GPA, and then handed him a job application.

The young man thanked Vest again, for everything. He said he didn't know how he could ever thank Vest enough for all he had done.

Vest held out his hand for a goodbye handshake and said, "You know how you can best thank me?"

The young man listened attentively.

Vest said, "Pay it forward."

He gave a gentle high five to the young man, then walked back into the stadium.

QUARTER1

CHAPTER 1

THE PERFECT DAY

SATURDAY MORNING

Ray Sonnen woke up Saturday morning to a perfect day. There was a gentle breeze and a bright blue sky, and the sun was as radiant as Ray at the thought of the first football game of the season. With a smile, he went through his morning routine of working out, getting the morning paper, and reading it over breakfast.

As he washed his breakfast dishes, Ray thought about an offer that had been made to him the day before. Over the last year, Ray had advised the executive management of a new company as it looked to grow. That company had just successfully closed a major round of funding. Subsequently, the company's young CEO had invited Ray to join the company's board of directors.

Ray had never served on a company's board before, and he was touched and intrigued by the invitation to do so. He generally worked with companies as a consultant for a predetermined period of time before moving on to his next client. He wanted to think about what it would be like to be involved with a company for a longer period of time.

After inviting Ray to join his company's board of directors, the CEO had said, "No need to give me a decision until you come back from your vacation."

A PREVIOUS WEEK'S MEMORY

The two men were talking at the company's funding celebration party, while surrounded by delighted and excited employees. Ray had gotten to know all of them over the past year. They were an energetic and motivated group of people, eager to succeed in their own careers and help the company be a success. That's why Ray, a popular and successful management and career consultant, had been brought on board. He was known for helping companies figure out the best ways to sustain a high level of growth and success.

The young CEO had continued talking about Ray's vacation. He added, "I know how much you're looking forward to the beach."

Ray had laughed and responded, "You're absolutely right. But you know I'll still be in town every Saturday for the game."

The young CEO had smiled thoughtfully. "I know," he said, finally. "You know … going to those games with you helped influence the way I lead the company, and the company is all the better for it. Thank you."

The two men had then parted with handshakes that rapidly turned into hugs and promises to tailgate together at some of the upcoming games.

Ray knew he would have plenty of time for relaxing at the beach. When he wasn't fishing, he would be reading in a hammock. He would see friends and, of course, drive back to town for the home games. Some away games would be within driving distance as well. There would be nothing tougher on the agenda than fishing, cooking delicious meals, and picking out what book to read next. He would be just as busy down at the beach as he would be working—he knew from long experience that someone like him couldn't just sit still and do nothing—but his energy would be devoted solely to fun and rejuvenating activities.

SATURDAY AFTERNOON

Ray glanced at his watch and decided to leave the rest of his packing for after the game. All he really needed to do was toss his electronics into the car. Everything else was already neatly packed up, ready to be unpacked at the beach.

It was warm enough out that Ray put down the top of his convertible as he drove to the stadium for the first game of the season.

Ray jogged up three wide steps to the path that led into the main stadium entry, while jingling the spare change in his pocket, a habit.

A young couple danced by Ray. Loudly, joyfully they chanted while dancing, "We're ready, we're ready, we're ready for the game, ready for the game, we're ready, we're ready, we're ready for the game!"

Other fans streaming by cheered them on, clapping and cheering as well.

The enthusiasm and energy of the people around him pulled at Ray. His steps quickened as he walked along the path into what he considered one of the happiest places in the world. Many other people thought about the stadium in the same way.

Statues of the school's sport heroes—legends who accomplished feats of seemingly mythic proportions—lined the path into the stadium. Only people who made a significant difference to the students and the school received the rare honor to have their statue commissioned; the last one had gone up almost a decade ago.

At an uncommon sight, Ray stopped. There were freshly turned dirt and newly planted flowers around the border of a new square of concrete.

"Wow," he thought, restarting his steps. "They're putting up a new statue." He wondered briefly who it would be. Traditionally, the statue was revealed at the last game of the season. Fans would spend the season guessing the identity of the person being honored.

As Ray entered the stadium, he caught sight of his mentor and season ticket seatmate and bellowed, "*Hey, Rock Star!*" Ray had developed his outdoor voice while working at different sport organizations in the beginning of his career. It carried.

A smiling older man in an athletic jersey acknowledged Ray with a grin and a nod before turning back to the family in front of him. As he got closer, Ray heard multiple generations of the family trying to get the man's attention.

"Please, let us get a word in edgewise and talk to Vest for a moment, honey," the silver-haired man said to his overexcited young granddaughter.

"Bob, you just give Miss Sophia a moment to tell Vest here all the details of her softball game," Vest said in a mock rebuke.

The proud grandfather and grandmother beamed, as did Sophia's parents, relieved to have Sophia's energy directed elsewhere. They were busy jointly tending to the young toddler twisting about in his mother's arms. The dad played defense, rapidly preparing a bottle to keep the toddler quiet while a tiny baby girl—miraculously sleeping through all the noise—stayed cuddled up in a baby sling across her father's chest.

Vest scooped Sophia up as she continued to happily talk to him.

Excitedly, she said, "I swung the bat, and I got a home run, and my friend Joyce swung the bat and she made it to second base …"

Sophia prattled airily at high volume. She was wholly confident in Vest's overwhelming interest in her detailed description of her last softball game.

Vest didn't let her down.

"Your friend Joyce," he said thoughtfully. "That's the one with the fish aquarium in her very own room, right?"

Vest had heard all about Joyce months ago, the last time Sophia had treated him to her postgame review.

Sophia's father looked at Vest in surprise. It was all he could do to remember the names and pets of his own kids, let alone the names of their friends, let alone what pets they had.

Sophia saw one of her friends enter the stadium and abruptly stopped her commentary at the third inning.

Vest set Sophia down, gently. "Go say hi to Thomas," he suggested.

Sophia sped off, with her dad and the sleeping baby girl in hot pursuit.

Vest turned toward Sophia's mom. "Helen!" he said, giving her a big hug.

"How are you doing with Bob Jr., there?" he asked, as he gently tickled the wide-eyed toddler under a milk-drenched chin. Helen, a pretty mom wearing the home team's colors, smiled widely at Vest. Before she could answer him, her parents took her daughter's place for Vest's attention.

"Vest!" Sophia's grandfather said anxiously. "I have to tell you about my new car."

"I know, Bob," Vest said, laughing. "It's a silver SC 430 convertible. And Maude here was super excited about you getting it too, right?"

Vest winked at Maude as she rolled her eyes and grinned. Vest knew she had told Bob up to the minute he drove the car home not to waste money on a new car. Vest also knew that she had dashed outside almost as quickly as Sophia could run to enjoy her first ride with the top down.

Sophia returned, tugging her slightly out-of-breath father by the hand, and Vest greeted the now-awake baby girl by name, earning another smile and a kiss from Helen before the entire family left for their seats, calling out their see-you-laters to Vest.

Ray knew he wouldn't get a chance to talk to Vest for a while. It was the first game of the season, and there were several more families headed Vest's way. Vest would greet each person by name and usually ask a question or two about their hobbies or interests, or mention a recent or upcoming birthday. Vest's memory was legendary. The only thing he was more well known for was his boundless love for every person who entered his stadium that he got to know. Some days, Ray thought, that seemed like every single person in the stadium.

Ray headed off to concessions to fuel up.

"Hey, Hal," Ray said, arriving at the counter and taking out his wallet.

"Ray," Hal said back. He waved Ray's wallet away, while quickly assembling an array of game food into a box.

"You see the boss up front?"

"Yes," said Ray, accepting a satisfyingly heavy tray of the type of food that only tastes really good at games. "Thank you, Hal!" Ray glanced down at the tray Hal had handed him. "Great job remembering the extra jalapenos on the nachos! And that I switched to lemonade from soda!"

Hal nodded and grinned.

"Yeah, I just saw the Rock Star," Ray said.

It was the name by which Vest was commonly known. All of Vest's former (Ray) and current (Hal) employees called Vest "Rock Star."

And most people at the receiving end of Vest's supernatural customer service thought Vest went beyond "Rock Star"—into the realm of reverence. Turning water into wine was all well and good. But pulling six tickets for seats together on the fifty-yard line on game day from his pocket, as Vest was known to do, was the type of modern-day miracle that could yank a hallelujah from folks who often sent their strongest prayers from the pew of the pigskin.

"Still greeting everyone by name, that showoff?" laughed Hal. He was already putting together a heavily loaded set of boxes of food for the next person.

"Four potato chips, four hot dogs, two packs of peanuts, and four soft drinks, for you, right, Jake?" Hal yelled out to the person standing behind Ray.

"You're far from a slouch yourself, Hal," Ray said, as he took his tray and made room for Jake.

Hal shrugged, pleased at the compliment. Ray said goodbye and headed to his seat with Vest.

As he walked to his seat, Ray thought about how some of his most joyous memories had taken place in the stadium he knew so well. He remembered the delight he had felt twenty years earlier, upon learning his part-time job in Vest's stadium would turn into a full-time position directly after graduation. Full-time exposure to Vest's management style was what Ray imagined a plant felt like after a day under the sun. Vest grew and nourished eager people who were ready to learn, but you had to be face forward at all times to get the full benefit. Vest was a firm believer in show, not tell. Ray was pretty sure that Vest had never once told Hal to try to remember the names and preferred orders for as many customers as possible. But Hal had somehow picked it up and started doing it anyway.

Ray could relate. He had picked up plenty from Vest during the five years he worked for him. The way that Vest thought about and did things was with the belief that any possible situation that could be made better should and would be. It wasn't a casual or simple thing. The university's stadium that Vest ran held tens of thousands of people. It was the largest employer on campus after the school itself, and thousands of town residents and current and former students filled it weekly.

In the beginning of working for Vest, Ray had tried to figure out if there was anything complex about Vest's successful leadership. Numerous people who had worked for Vest went on to very successful careers. And the stadium was known nationwide for creating a level of happiness normally associated with Disneyland. Ray ultimately reminded himself that Vest's leadership style was no less wise or remarkably effective for being simple to understand.

Vest was still surrounded by and effortlessly conversing with adoring families. Ray waved at him and made his way to their seats, still lost in memory. He thought back to the day he had told Vest of his career plan for life.

PAST MEMORIES

Ray had received a job offer to run the sport organization at another, smaller university. He couldn't imagine not working for Vest.

"Working at this stadium is the best job I'll ever have," Ray had said. Then he had added, "I'm never going to work anywhere other than here or for anyone else other than you."

After Ray said that, Vest looked at him thoughtfully. "Well," Vest said finally, leaning forward. "What if I fire you instead?"

Far too kind to let Ray experience more than a split second of horror, Vest had immediately explained that the job offer represented a great opportunity for Ray to operate as the head of a sport organization, rather than second in command.

It had taken hours of conversation and convincing before Ray agreed to accept the leadership position of the sport organization at the smaller university.

In his new leadership role, Ray had quickly gained a reputation for supernatural customer service, a passionate work ethic, and continually inspiring employees of his own to new heights of service and success. One season ticket holder, a good friend of the college's president, learned that thanks to Ray's new initiatives and leadership, the revenue from the entire sport organization had nearly doubled. The season ticket holder was also the business professor at the university. She asked Ray to come and talk to her class of aspiring MBAs. That was the first time Ray had written down the four main principles he had learned from Vest as crucial for good leadership.

Ray thought that the MBA students probably remembered the explosive revenue-growth chart he showed more than the four principles he discussed. Whatever it was they remembered, they had gone on to invite him to talk to managers and employees at the companies they had founded or were tapped to run. Start-ups, nonprofits, established corporations, and sport franchises all wanted the same thing: to achieve more, better than they ever had before, by hiring only the best people. Ray's leadership counseling became well known for inspiring employees to unheard-of heights of creativity, collaboration, customer satisfaction, and bottom-line financial success.

He had expanded his principles chart to link to the concepts he was teaching. Ray was pleased that the first letter of each of the concepts spelled out Vest's name. It made sense.

PRINCIPLES:

IMAGINE

INVOLVE

INFORM

INSPIRE

VALUE

EMPOWER

SCORE

TRAIN

Are You All In? Ray reflected his positive sports-oriented personality into a short tagline he'd write under the chart. "Are you all in?" he would ask, after explaining the principles and concepts that made for the strongest and consistently energized workforce.

People would say loudly in response to Ray's question, "*All in!*"

BACK IN THE PRESENT— SATURDAY AFTERNOON

With the game about to start, Ray watched Vest make his way to their seats. Vest was still greeting everyone he passed by name, giving high fives, handshakes, kisses, and hugs until he reached their row.

"ENERGYMAN!" Vest cried out, with a huge smile and at top volume. "How're you doing?"

Ray blushed only slightly. It was a nickname he not-so-secretly enjoyed, even employing it on his popular website, where CEOs of high-powered companies fell over themselves to have their testimonials posted. He thought of ENERGYMAN as his superhero alter ego.

The CEO of a company whose app was one of the most downloaded of all time had gratefully written about his experience with Ray, saying, "When Ray comes into a room, he vanquishes the villains that keep people from feeling or performing their best. Everyone becomes more energized. What's more, they all stay that way! It's like Ray leaves some magical, permanent source of energy behind. Everyone at our company now just calls him 'ENERGYMAN.'"

Ray liked the villains example as much as he liked his superhero nickname. He had a list of common traits he found in companies that needed help reenergizing their workforce. Calling those traits "villains" and naming them "the Reaction Gang" was easy. They were apathy, chaos, defeat, fear, negativity, procrastination, and blind adherence to the status quo. Like germs or viruses left untreated, those adverse traits would make a company sick or low performing in the same way illnesses made people tired—they depleted energy. ENERGYMAN had great fun in vaporizing or preventing those villains from taking hold. So did Ray. The list of villains was always found at any struggling organization.

In fact, they were out in full force at a local company that had recently reached out to Ray for help. Ray wanted to talk to Vest about that company. He planned to do so at this game.

"ENERGYMAN says sit down—the game's about to start," Ray said, and he handed Vest his drink.

Vest smiled and slung his right arm around Ray's shoulder, giving him a bro-hug hello. Both men had their eyes glued to the field as the game began. Ray was smiling too. He was content to be sitting next to the man he admired most at the first game of the season.

Ray was even happier than usual, since the next morning he would be driving to the beach for an extended time away from work. ENERGYMAN, he thought, needed to recharge his own batteries before the next gig, which, like all the others, was sure to be intense. For now, there was a home-team game that needed to be won.

CHAPTER 2
IN VEST
WE TRUST

When the halftime whistle blew, everyone at the game was in even higher spirits, thanks to a stunning Hail Mary pass and field goal that turned a tie into a seven-point lead for the home team.

Ray had just finished telling Vest his plans for his time off.

Vest said, "You know, I'm always proud of you. I have been since the day you started working for me and it was clear you were going to do whatever you could, whenever you could, to make a situation for someone even better. You've more than earned this time off. I know you'll enjoy it."

Ray looked at the field.

"Vest," he said, in an uncharacteristically quiet voice, "do you think we always have to take an opportunity to make things better, even if we don't want to or if the time isn't right for us?"

Vest said, "What's on your mind, Ray?"

This was what Ray had wanted to talk to Vest about. He wasn't sure there would be enough time before the second half of the game started. Before Ray could keep talking, Vest gestured to him, and they made their way to Vest's private office. It was decked out with everything the man needed to keep his eye on the game and the stands. The two men would be able to watch the game and, equally important, anyone who needed to contact Vest could do so in a second. Calling it a private office was kind of a joke. Vest practiced a completely open-door policy. Anyone who wanted to look in, to talk to or to learn from Vest, was welcome to do so and often did. Vest's office was as much of a classroom as any other on campus. In his office and stadium his employees learned what Vest taught: practical wisdom.

When they walked into Vest's office, Ray saw a pile of large poster-board cards stacked up in one corner, reminding him of another teaching technique he borrowed from Vest over the years. Were there any lessons, Ray wondered, that he taught that he hadn't initially learned from Vest?

Ray and Vest sat down in front of the massive flat-screen TV with the sound on mute.

Ray said, "I'm struggling with an opportunity that seems like a no-brainer not to accept." He continued, "I just finished a long and intense gig, I've been looking forward to my vacation for a really long time, and I definitely need to recharge my batteries. Saying no is obviously the right choice, but something about saying no just feels … wrong, somehow. I can't figure it out."

Vest said, "Tell me about it."

Ray then explained that about a month earlier a headhunter had called to sound him out about a job opportunity at Energy Production Company, locally known as EPC.

Until recently it was the region's biggest success story: founded by the son of a local businessman known as Mr. Lyre, who was as autocratic as his son was democratic. Brian, the company's founder, was a brilliant person with multiple degrees in engineering, physics, and business who had founded EPC along with his best friend, John. Both men contributed to the strong success of the company. John was the wizard who dreamed up theories of energy production and then turned them into practical, low-cost solutions, and Brian was the networker and practical manager who hired well and secured a record first round of funding to support more research and development and hiring. Brian's last big accomplishment was opening a building that would house the production of an EPC model that would strengthen and expand the reach of the region's aging electricity grid, while at the same time lowering bills for the company's customers.

The night before the company planned to open its new industrial production warehouse with a big party, John had driven out to give the on-site machines a final check to make sure everything would run smoothly on the first day. The company's decision to keep the manufacturing facility in the region would create thousands of new jobs. It was a huge deal that everyone was excited about.

It was a windy, rainy night when John drove up to the facility. He saw that the door was open and irregular flashes of light were arcing across the machines inside. He quickly put on protective gloves and ran indoors, where he found Brian lying dead on the floor. Brian had been hiding prizes, one for each employee, throughout the facility. The prizes were all the same: a key to a stand-alone safety deposit box, designed in the shape of the new EPC model that was to be built at the facility. Brian had hidden a single key at each employee's workstation, and the boxes were all lined up waiting in the room where the party was to take place. In each box was a stock certificate, made out to each employee, for one thousand shares of EPC. It was the classic, classy, thoughtful, kind, and generous gesture Brian was known for. Unfortunately, as he was twisting one of the final keys into a wire that would hang down into a welder's workstation, he slipped. The wire he was holding tore and brushed by an open socket, instantly electrocuting Brian. The ambulance was called, but there was no resuscitating Brian. The party was canceled, as were the plans to build the EPC model. EPC still existed—Brian's father, Mr. Lyre, had taken over as CEO a month after his son's untimely passing— but the manufacturing facility remained closed.

Ray explained to Vest what the headhunter had asked him. "She told me that before Brian and John's energy accelerator invention, the company had a solid foundation supplying electricity in the traditional way to customers in the region. Mr. Lyre doesn't want anything to do with the model John and Brian invented. He told the employees who were supposed to work in the facility that he would buy back their shares or they could take jobs in the company's call center."

Vest asked, "How did that work out for Mr. Lyre and EPC?"

Ray answered slowly, "It depends on your point of view, I guess." He was disturbed to share this next bit of news. "I've heard that Mr. Lyre says the stock buyback offer worked out great because those shares cost him nothing to buy back from people who didn't want to stay at EPC … and that the people who wanted to keep their shares while working in the call center almost always quit in under a year, so they lost their shares, regardless."

Both men sat quietly, thinking that it was odd and disturbing to hear the father of a man who had so tragically lost his life describe what sounded like the undoing of one of his son's last and most gracious acts as "working out great."

"Anyway," Ray continued, "the headhunter said the board had pitched me to Mr. Lyre as a 'co-CEO.' Evidently he won't give up the CEO title—says it has something to do with keeping it within the family. You know my doctrine; 'coleader' is basically the same as 'no leader.' I told her that I'd rarely known of a successful coleading situation. Even Brian and John had clearly outlined roles and responsibilities."

Ray summed up, "So in the last nine months or so, many people have left the company. Some of the early employees, including John, stayed, and he and others are still hoping to convince Mr. Lyre to go back to the creative new initiatives that his son had put in place. However, Mr. Lyre is autocratic and has an old-school style as a manager. Evidently, he likes to demand better results on reduced budgets without being bothered with the details. And in the early days of his tenure, he managed to stack the board of directors with enough of his old cronies that he can't easily be unseated, despite the fact the company is stagnating and losing market share and has a plummeting stock price."

Ray sighed and then shared the headhunter's ask on behalf of EPC's board of directors.

"They want me to come in as president and turn the place around." He looked up at Vest, unsure. "From what I've heard, EPC is overrun with villains. And this energyman needs some time at the beach to regain his ALL CAPS status. Am I wrong? Am I being selfish? What do you think?"

Vest sat and thought. The game had ended, with a home-team win, and his stadium was still humming as fans milled around happily and employees were busily cleaning the place up.

Vest said, "I can understand someone not wanting to take on the combination of a status quo CEO and a bunch of disengaged employees at any time, let alone right after coming off of a busy and intense job, like you just had."

Ray was already nodding when a small warning sound went off in the back of his head. Had he really thought Vest would agree to him going down to the beach to bury his head in the sand for three months?

Vest dug into one of his pockets and pulled something out, scattering a handful of coins across the table in front of the two men. Ray leaned forward.

That's odd, Ray thought. Three of the coins seemed to be actually glowing.

"Do you trust me?" Vest asked.

Ray almost laughed before he saw how seriously Vest expected him to consider that question.

"Vest," Ray said, "I trust you more than anyone in my life."

Silently, he said to himself, And that will never, ever change.

CHAPTER 3
DISBELIEF

SATURDAY, EARLY EVENING

Ray looked closer at the coins Vest had spread out on the table in front of them. Among the usual scattering of quarters, dimes, nickels, and pennies, there were three coins that were unlike any Ray had ever seen before. They were glowing. As Vest began talking, the coins seemed to shine even more brightly.

"These are Unbelievium coins," Vest said.

"That makes sense … because I can't *believe* what I'm seeing!" Ray said. He couldn't figure out what was making the coins glow.

The coins dimmed noticeably at Ray's comment, and his jaw dropped.

Vest laughed. "Do you believe what you just saw?"

The coins were glowing brightly again.

Ray wanted to say he wasn't sure, but he didn't want to be responsible for dimming the coins' bright glow. More importantly, Ray wasn't in the habit of not believing Vest. He certainly wasn't going to start now.

Vest said again, "These are Unbelievium coins."

Ray stayed quiet.

Vest said, "Most people can give you millions of reasons why something *won't* work."

Ray nodded. He was more than familiar with that particular aspect of human nature. It was especially true of people working at a company that wasn't doing well, regardless of whether they were employees, managers, or the CEO. You'd think they'd be willing to try almost anything to make things better.

Defeatism, demotivation, and reactiveness were common traits at poorly performing companies—they could infect an office as fast as the common cold and were just as hard to get rid of. But it could be done with good hygiene—whether it was handwashing or simply letting in some bright sunlight and positive energy to disinfect a place. Regardless, when a body was tired and down, it was easier to sink into negativity and come up with reasons something wouldn't work, rather than figure out how to make something work. Summoning up the energy and creativity to think of and try something new was especially hard for people who weren't feeling good about where they were or what their leaders or their companies were doing.

Vest reached over and picked up one of the many cue cards that were stacked neatly along the side of his desk. He held it up to Ray and asked, "What does it say?"

The card, the size of a poster board, had a single word on it that Ray read out loud. "Imagine."

Ray had seen this card before, held up by Vest. And, of course, Ray had borrowed the concept in his own leadership training sessions. When Ray held up his cue card, he would ask his listeners to imagine the type of value they could create. Often, people took that to mean monetary value. A few more thoughtful leaders took that to mean imagine how to lead in a way that constantly inspired and created other leaders. However, Ray knew that for Vest, asking someone to imagine something could, and often did, go beyond just imagining a winning game, season, or prize.

Vest took things to their ultimate end. If something was worth doing, in Vest's world, it wasn't just worth doing well—as the saying went. For Vest, if something was worth doing, it was worth doing superlatively well. Supernaturally well. So incredibly well that people would remember it and feel inspired by it.

Ray looked at the sign and back down at the table, where the three Unbelievium coins were still glowing. As far as he knew, there wasn't a metal that glowed like that. Was he imagining this? Had Vest imagined the Unbelievium coins into existence? And if so, why weren't they called something like Imaginarium coins? What was the purpose of these coins, and why was Vest showing them to him?

Vest said, "I think that people sometimes have to believe in the unbelievable."

Ray had heard Vest say that before.

Then Vest said, "Here, hold on to these."

He scooped the coins up and handed them to Ray, who, used to doing what Vest asked him to do, accepted them.

"Let me walk you out to your car," Vest said to Ray. "I know you have a lot to do tonight."

Ray wondered whether there was more to that sentence. Did Vest mean in terms of packing up so that Ray could head down to the beach the next day? Or did he mean something else?

The two men talked for a short while more at Ray's car before saying goodbye.

Ray got into his car and drove home. He kept the top of the hardtop convertible up, blocking out the rays of the setting sun.

QUARTER2

CHAPTER 4
UNBELIEVIUM

SATURDAY NIGHT

Back at his house, Ray sat down in his home office at his desk. He routinely tossed the loose change from his pockets into a glass jar on top of his desk, this time with the Unbelievium coins among them. He tilted his chair back and thought about the afternoon. He could barely remember the game itself, which was a shame, since it was evidently a great one to kick off the season. His mind was too full.

Vest never missed an opportunity to do something for someone else. Especially someone in need. And since whatever Vest did for someone else left them feeling thoroughly taken care of, they never forgot him or what he said when they thanked him.

He said to pay it forward.

Vest hadn't said he thought Ray should take the job of president at EPC. He had asked Ray, matter-of-factly, what he traditionally felt to be more energizing: working hard or hanging out at the beach. It was clear what Vest was driving at.

Ray knew he had talents. Some of his talents were gifts, and others were skills. Both benefited from the training he got working for Vest. Ray had always known how to work hard and go that extra mile. But he hadn't always known how to direct his energy until he began working for Vest. When he started as a manager, he definitely didn't know how to inspire hard work in others. Until he started working for Vest, Ray thought of people as hard workers or not hard workers. It never occurred to him that people who didn't work hard were that way not because they were lazy but because they didn't feel empowered or proud of what they were being asked to do. In working for Vest, Ray saw how Vest—time and time again—helped people take initiative, and pride, in their hard work and achievements.

Vest had listened to Ray talk about why he wanted the time off rather than go work for EPC. He suggested that Ray write down all the accomplishments of the job he had finished, which ones he was most proud of, and then prioritize them.

Ray figured this would be easy, since keeping track of performance by metrics was something he tracked on every job, and those numbers were easily accessible on his computer. That part took only thirty minutes, and the list included items such as these:

- Helped secure record Series A funding round of $200 million

- Increased employee satisfaction rate from 75 percent to 98 percent

- Drove customer call center satisfaction rate Net Promoter Score (NPS) to 9 and 10 from 6 and 7

- Increased production by 15 percent

- Increase sales (new product) by 40 percent

Those were all great numbers, Ray thought. They represented impressive increases across almost every single important metric. But he wasn't directly responsible for them, so how could he be proud of them?

Ray stared at the list some more. He knew the funding results came from the hours he spent working with the CEO, asking him to imagine what could be possible. He was prouder of the night they made a major breakthrough—the point where the CEO stopped saying, "But that's never been done before," and started agreeing to imagine what it would be like if what they were talking about could be done.

Ray looked at the increase in call center customer satisfaction rates. That didn't come from any study on the internet or management book. He had taken all of the call center employees out to a game at Vest's stadium, where they had seen the football coaches use poster board cue cards during the game, with great success. When Ray had next gone into the call center, he found decorated poster boards by each desk. Evidently everyone, not just weekend workers, had come in with their own supplies to decorate and kick off a friendly competition using inspiring signs as well as mountains of confetti, gift certificate codes that could be given to customers, and a daily leaderboard of operators with the highest satisfaction scores by callers.

The poster board idea had come from a regular operator named Mark, and his manager, Robyn, who supported him by reimbursing everyone's expenses and investing in prizes. Ray was really proud of her after she told him she imagined what could make work more fun and successful was the same poster board system she had seen used at the stadium.

Ray looked over the list with new awareness, and he realized that what he was most proud of were the people who had made those achievements possible. He hadn't told them what to do. He did know that simply telling people what to do almost never worked. What he was most proud of was helping people find the energy and opportunity to imagine what they could do better for themselves, their coworkers, and their company and putting those ideas into sustainable practice.

Ray thought back to the young CEO of the company, who asked him to join the board. He had said going to a game with Ray had changed the way he led the company, but he hadn't elaborated.

A RECENT MEMORY

Ray remembered the first game he had taken that CEO to.

When Ray and the CEO had entered the stadium together, Ray had steered them toward a crowd of smiling people. The group of happy people were surrounding a man the CEO had assumed was a well-known football player whose autograph they wanted or maybe a selfie for their social media. Of course, it was Vest. And as they had drawn closer to Vest, the CEO had seen that Vest was busy handing out what Ray had explained were what Vest called "Jesus Tickets."

The CEO had asked if they were religious in some way.

"No," Ray had replied. "Jesus Tickets are the game-day tickets that Vest holds aside for special purposes, at every single game. Sometimes he uses them for friends of the president or VIPs like politicians, who show up unannounced when the stadium is sold out."

Ray had continued, "Vest most often uses Jesus Tickets for regular fans. People who have a family of six but only managed to find four seats together, for example. Vest will just yank out six tickets on the fifty-yard line and hand them over. Or he'll just go up and wander in the top section and find people who are at their very first game and then escort them down to seats near the players' entrance to the stadium so the kids can high-five players."

The CEO had asked, "How many tickets does he carry at any given time?"

Ray had been able to answer without even thinking about it, because the number never changed. "He always carries at least fifty. It doesn't matter if it is a regular season game or a playoff game. Vest will use those tickets to make a good situation better or to make up for a bad situation—either way, the power those tickets have to change someone's experience is practically supernatural."

The CEO had asked Ray what he meant by supernatural.

Ray had thought a bit before answering.

Ray had finally said, "I guess I mean out-of-this-world magically good. Going above and beyond what is normal or expected. Service that transcends what people thought could be possible. When Vest uses the tickets to make something better, people don't accept the tickets as something due to them … they walk away far, far happier than they were before. Most of the time, when there's an issue, people seem to expect a fix rather than be thankful for it. Vest's Jesus Tickets seem to always make people much happier than you'd think a simple fix could make them. It's pretty impressive."

The CEO had remained quiet for the rest of that game and in the following week spent a lot of time in the office with his CFO and legal team. Ray began to hear stories of cards left on different people's desks. The cards would have a handwritten note and an official ten-share block of stock made out in that person's name.

Ray, respecting the CEO's desire to make that his own practice, had been quietly proud to watch it unfold and take root. People at that company did a good job because they loved to do a good job and inspire each other. But if Ray had to think of one thing that he was most proud of seeing occur during his time with that CEO, it was that quiet, thoughtful custom. All employees of the company were already shareholders, a practice both the CEO and Ray thought was critical to employee engagement. But the added extra perk combined with the personal, handwritten note definitely had the element of the supernatural about it. Like a grown-up tooth fairy that was the stock fairy.

Remembering that story made Ray think of Brian, the original founder and CEO of EPC. He also had automatically made his employees shareholders. And it was his desire to give them more stock that resulted in his fatal accident. Ray frowned as he thought of what he heard about Mr. Lyre, that the man had bought back the original employees' shares for pennies on the dollar. It was hardly in keeping with the values of the company his son had founded.

SATURDAY NIGHT

Ray drew a deep breath, bringing his mind back to the present.

Vest's question to Ray was at the top of his mind—what would energize Ray more? Taking on a new work challenge or lying around at the beach?

Before Ray drove home, Vest had written something down on a piece of paper and folded it twice before handing it to Ray.

"What do you want me to do with this?" Ray had asked.

Vest had said, "Put it on your bedside table, and open it as soon as you wake up tomorrow morning."

It was close to midnight when Ray decided to turn in.

When he woke up the next morning, the sun was shining. Ray thought he should have felt like leaping out of bed, tossing the last few items he needed for the beach into his car, and heading out. Instead, he reached over slowly and unfolded the paper Vest had handed him late yesterday afternoon.

It said: Have you started unpacking yet?

SUNDAY AFTERNOON

To: Holly Headhunter (holly@headhunter.com)

cc: EPC BOD (boardofdirectors@epc.com);
   Mr. Lyre (lyresr@epc.com)

bcc: ENERGYMAN (energyman@raysonnenphd.org)

Dear Holly and Team,

Thank you taking the time to meet with me during this last month to share your thoughts, goals, and ideas about Energy Production Company (EPC)'s next phase. It is heartening that the board is considering reinstating the foundational components upon which Brian originally started EPC. That is in large part why I would like to accept the role of president of EPC, reporting to Mr. Lyre (CEO).

I understand and respect the importance of balancing Mr. Lyre's management style with the agreed-upon goals of the board and me, and I appreciate your faith in my ability to navigate both thoughtfully and effectively. I hope Mr. Lyre and I will be able to have several useful conversations before I start full time next month.

In the meantime, thank you again for your support and enthusiasm. I look forward to working for you, Mr. Lyre, the shareholders, and employees of EPC, as we embark on the journey begun by Brian with the intent of fulfilling his ultimate goals.

With warm regards,
Ray Sonnen

CHAPTER 5

THE TIP OF
THE ICEBERG

TWO WEEKS LATER—
SATURDAY AFTERNOON

"It's game day!" yelled Vest, as he held up a hand for a high five.

"I know," grumbled Ray, half-heartedly high-fiving Vest back. "It's also freezing! Wasn't the sun shining just recently?"

"Oh please," Vest said. "You've been far colder than this. Forget about the weather, ENERGYMAN. Tell me about your new job starting next week."

Ray stifled a sigh but wasn't able to entirely hold back on the sass.

"You mean the job I took to turn around a company where the employees are miserable, the CEO is clueless, the customers are leaving by droves, and the stock price is in the toilet instead of spending three months at the beach? That job?"

Vest just glanced at Ray, and Ray immediately straightened up. He knew Vest had asked him a serious question and wanted to know all about what Ray would be doing when he started his new job next week.

Ray said, "In all seriousness, I'm worried."

"Why?" asked Vest, surprised. "What's different about this company from the other companies in tough spots that you've helped before?"

Ray listed a few things: This time he wouldn't be a consultant but a full-time employee without an end date, whereas normally Ray took on gigs ranging anywhere from three months to one year. It would also be a situation where the CEO was on record as not seeing a problem to be fixed—Ray was being brought on by the board of directors and would be reporting to the CEO, the very man who didn't want him and didn't believe there was anything that needed to be improved. And finally, Ray summed up, he had never gone into a company with less insight into numbers—performance metrics—than this one.

"How is that possible?" asked Vest. "Didn't the board give you all the data you asked for?"

"Well," said Ray, "that's part of the issue. Mr. Lyre has stacked the board with enough of his friends that each decision ends in an effective deadlock. The board members who wanted me on board were able to hire me because of a threat by an activist shareholder. Mr. Lyre had told the board when he first took over as CEO that he would submit internal numbers once a year and that the quarterly numbers shared with the board would be the same as those shared with the market. It is an unorthodox way of managing a company, but the respect around Brian's death and the company's relatively low presence kind of let the situation slide far longer than it would have otherwise."

Vest cut to the chase.

He asked, "So what does that mean for you, specifically?"

Ray said, "It means I'm going in essentially blind. I have the public numbers, which are all trending down. The only numbers trending up are the bad ones: customers leaving, employee dissatisfaction, employee turnover, negative reviews on employee sites."

Ray added, "Here's another number for you: seven."

"Seven?" Vest asked. "What does that mean?"

Ray grimaced.

"That's the number of times Sammy Sidewinder—yes, that's his real name, Mr. Lyre's executive assistant—has made and then canceled calls or meetings I had scheduled with Mr. Lyre. The first time I'll be actually meeting and speaking with the CEO of EPC, the man to whom I'll be reporting, is on Monday, my first day of work." Ray took a deep breath and said, "It is pretty unbelievable."

"Oh!" Vest said brightly. "That reminds me. Don't forget to bring those Unbelievium coins I gave you into the office with you every day. High five!"

Vest held up his hand.

Ray just looked at him.

SUNDAY EVENING

Before Ray headed up to bed on Sunday night, he finished writing a list of thoughts and reminders for his first day at the office. He placed his list by the other items he needed to take with him the next day—his cell phone, his two government forms of ID, personal knickknacks and pictures for his desk, and his personal laptop for IT to install the company email on. It was the same list and items he always used before the start of every new work engagement.

The Unbelievium coins had entirely slipped Ray's mind. They were still in the glass jar on Ray's desk among his other loose change.

MONDAY MORNING— RAY'S FIRST DAY AT EPC

Ray stood in front of Sammy Sidewinder's desk, in front of Mr. Lyre's closed office door. Unbelievably, the executive assistant had a name tag that confirmed this was his real name and not a joke. Even more unbelievably, he hadn't stood up or even acknowledged Ray.

That was not okay.

Before Ray was ENERGYMAN, he worked exclusively for sport organizations, where the ability to make oneself heard across large spaces and among noisy crowds was a key skill.

"GOOD MORNING!" Ray boomed down at Sammy, as if the man were sitting at a desk halfway across a football field, instead of two feet in front of him.

The assistant jumped and then hissed with surprise as he fell out of his chair.

"Good morning," Sammy said sulkily, as he stood up.

"I didn't see you standing there," he added, insincerely.

Ray smiled at Sammy and said, "I'm looking forward to speaking with Mr. Lyre."

Sammy knocked on Mr. Lyre's door. He stuck his head in to announce Ray's arrival. Instead of politely holding the door open, Sammy let the door start to swing shut. Ray shrugged and strode into Mr. Lyre's office, politely closing the door behind him before walking over to Mr. Lyre with his hand outstretched.

"Good morning, Mr. Lyre," Ray said.

"Yes," Mr. Lyre said. "I heard you say that from the other side of the door. Just sit down, young man. No need to shake hands or stand on ceremony."

Ray was surprised not to have his handshake accepted by Mr. Lyre, who showed no signs of standing up to greet him or move to the conference table in the office, where the two of them could speak more comfortably. Instead, it appeared Mr. Lyre would be holding this meeting with Ray sitting in an uncomfortable chair, while Mr. Lyre rested on a comfortable padded chair behind a large dark wood desk.

"Unfortunately," Mr. Lyre said, "I have an extremely busy day in front of me, so this won't be a long meeting. I understand you've been brought on at other companies before to help crack the whip and get employees back in their place and producing. How long do you think it'll take you to do that here?"

Ray was startled.

He said, "That's an interesting way of describing it. Generally, what I've done in previous engagements is spend time understanding a company's mission and foundational principles, what the organization values. Then I do a lot of research into the numbers beyond the bottom line—"

Mr. Lyre interrupted, "There aren't any numbers beyond the bottom line that I'm aware of."

Ray resumed, "Oh, numbers like performance metrics, employee satisfaction, customer satisfaction, all those types of numbers that can help—"

Mr. Lyre interrupted again.

"I don't care about any of those numbers," he said flatly.

Ray paused, then said, "In fact, those are numbers that can help improve the bottom line."

Mr. Lyre paused briefly, then snapped, "What do you mean?"

As Ray drew breath to answer, Mr. Lyre said, "Oh, forget it. I don't want to be bothered with details. I just tell my executives to figure out what to do, to do it well, and not bother me with all the details. After all, that's why they're making the big bucks. Isn't it?"

Ray said, "I get that you're tight on time and would like to keep this conversation big picture. How about I tell you a little bit about the 'pay it forward' strategy that I've seen pay off well for other organizations?"

Unwittingly, Ray had hit another one of Mr. Lyre's hot buttons.

"Pay it forward? Pay it forward?" Mr. Lyre said. "Spare me. I pay it forward," Mr. Lyre continued, speaking loudly.

"I pay it forward right into the pockets of every person in this office, and they take it home with them at the end of the day. Those people out there are just lucky to have jobs, is how I see it. That should be the full extent of any paying it forward from my end— that they get a paycheck. None of them stay around long enough to benefit from owning stock. And eliminating the paperwork for the employee stock share program alone has saved this company a tremendous amount of money. That benefited the bottom line!"

EPC had gone public less than three months before Brian died, and his death had sent the stock price to an all-time low, from where it had barely moved since. As a public company, EPC's financial statements were available online, and Ray had reviewed them all in detail. He knew that any money the company saved by eliminating the employee stock share program was likely dwarfed by the amount of money the company had lost on new marketing programs to win back lost customers, refunds due to overlong repair times, emergency repairs that had increased because Mr. Lyre had eliminated all but the most critical maintenance-check programs, and fines paid out to regulatory bodies who kept finding EPC maintenance workers without current certifications working in the field.

Ray realized that the demoralization of EPC employees was probably far worse than he imagined when he first decided to accept the position. That would make sense, he thought, given the words and actions of EPC's CEO, Mr. Lyre.

Ray left his meeting with Mr. Lyre more determined than ever to make a difference at EPC.

It was likely, he thought, going to be a far harder job than he imagined.

RAY'S FIRST WEEK AT EPC

Ray spent the rest of the week meeting with different leaders throughout the organization as well as walking around the company, introducing himself to as many employees as possible. Each night after he got home, he would set his phone by the front door and then dump his loose change into the glass jar on his desk. Then he would go work out before returning to his home office to write down his thoughts from the day and update his goals list for the next.

Each night, after he turned off his desk lamp, he would put his to-do list on the table near the front door, next to his phone, wallet, and keys. Ray liked to be able to scoop everything up quickly on his way out of the house each morning.

And each night the Unbelievium coins sent a very faint glow across his desk, visible only after Ray had turned off his lamp to leave the room.

So he never noticed them.

CHAPTER 6

TRIALS AND TRIBULATIONS

SATURDAY AFTERNOON

It was drizzling on Saturday, and Ray was already in a gray mood before he reached his office. Before he had driven to the game, he had dug out the list Vest had asked him to write of the things he was most proud of from previous job engagements. As he sat at his desk, looking the list over, it occurred to him to try to map each accomplishment to a characteristic he admired of Vest's. After all, it was first and always Vest who inspired Ray's management style.

Ray thought again about the CEO he had taken to a football game, the one who had been inspired to start his own thoughtful practice based on Vest's Jesus Tickets. That was a characteristic response to Vest's supernatural customer service, which often inspired people to try to re-create for other people how Vest made them feel: loved and valued and taken care of. Vest had inspired the CEO to leave handwritten notes to different employees for different reasons, sometimes just because they needed a boost or in thanks and recognition of a job well done.

Then, Ray thought about the first game of the season a few weeks ago, the only one he'd attended where the daily issues at EPC hadn't been weighing on him. Ray remembered Vest greeting multiple generations of families by name, giving them hugs and high fives, remembering their hobbies and their friends, showing them in any number of different ways how much he cared about them, how much he loved them. And Ray remembered seeing similar practices by Hal, the concessions stand worker, who remembered everyone's name and order. Ray thought that what both men did went beyond naturally good customer service. When remembering people—their names, their likes, their lives—Vest and Hal made people feel loved.

Ray looked down at what he had written:

- Fall in love with what you do

- Provide supernatural service

But as Ray looked over his list, it seemed there was something missing. There was an element that enabled Vest to teach without telling, that inspired and taught people to lead others in the same way.

Ray wrote down,

- Grow your genius

That, he thought, was a good way to describe what Vest inspired in others. He didn't tell people what to do. He showed, by example, the benefits of making people feel loved, by being remembered and taken care of. And his employees figured out how to do that in their own way.

Ray liked to wander the halls of places he worked in the late afternoons and early evenings. He always made a point to greet and talk to people he had met with earlier in the day or was scheduled to meet with later that week. He would thank them for a conversation they had or tell them how much he was looking forward to talking to them soon. That was a practice people always commented on—it wasn't so much that they remembered what he said, they would write to Ray, but that they remembered how Ray had made them feel.

One thank-you note an employee had written to Ray said, "Your seemingly simple act of referencing our conversations made me feel seen, heard, and valued. By the end, I would look forward not to our meetings but those casual 'looking forward to speaking with you' and 'that was a really helpful conversation earlier' conversations far more. They left me feeling inspired. I always felt a glow of satisfaction and intensity, I would strive to work harder, and I'd leave work not feeling exhausted but inspired to get in and do a great job the next day as well."

The gray rainy day made Ray notice that his home office was getting dim; it was hard for him to easily read the list he was working on. Ray rubbed his eyes and then opened them as he reached forward to switch on his desk lamp. He stopped in surprise—the list was now easy to see, even though a moment ago he could barely see it in the darkening room. But it was still raining hard and gray outside. Puzzled, Ray looked at his desk more carefully. He saw that there was a small glow coming from the glass jar on his desk—it was that glow that had lit up his list.

The memory of Vest's request at the football game came flooding back. Vest had asked Ray to bring the Unbelievium coins into the office with him every day. Ray was still unclear why, but he was deter-mined not to forget the Unbelievium coins again. He dug them out of the glass jar on his desk. Holding the coins in his hand, Ray studied them as they continued to glow gently. Ray got up and placed the three Unbelievium coins on the table near the front door so he would remember to take them to the office on Monday.

The rain outside slowed to a gentle drizzle.

LATER THAT AFTERNOON

Ray left for the game, putting on his jacket as he headed out to the car.

As usual, Ray got to the game early in an effort to spend time with Vest before the man's crowd of admirers descended.

This time, he got there early enough to watch the coaches of the visiting team slip clear plastic protectors over the poster-board signs that they held up for players. These signs were unique to every team and consisted of words or images that made sense only to that team's players. It was a fun game to try to figure out what the signs could mean.

As Ray stared at the poster boards, he remembered the ones he and Vest had seen over the years for home and visiting teams.

He started to think first if, then how, a practice like those poster-board signs could be used at EPC.

Ray was so deep in thought that he didn't notice when Vest sat down beside him.

"What are you thinking about?" Vest asked, with his customary, honest interest. When Vest asked a question to anyone, he meant it sincerely. It was never just casual social interaction.

Ray answered just as honestly. "You. And those signs," he said, gesturing to the field.

"Not work?" Vest asked.

It was a fair question. Almost all of their conversations lately had to do with EPC. At the last game, Ray had despairingly told Vest, "The gang's all here," when Vest asked about how things were at the office.

"Well," Ray said thoughtfully, "I think it might have to do with work after all, but in a good way."

Vest was relieved to hear it.

Some of the stories that Ray had shared with Vest over the past few weeks were upsetting.

For example, there were a few contract call center employees who held contests to see who could keep customers on hold the longest before they gave up and hung up. There were workers in the field who were so demotivated by long hours and low pay that they had begun using company laptops and cars to work on side gigs. Ray told Vest that he overheard some workers talking about how they made as much or more from their side gigs using the company resources.

The parking lot at EPC was almost completely empty by 5:00 p.m. every day. In fact, Ray had told Vest incredulously, it seemed the CEO himself, Mr. Lyre, left for lunch at noon each day and never came back to the office until nine the next morning. And no one ever saw Sammy Sidewinder at the office or received an email from him after 1:00 p.m.

It didn't surprise Ray, or Vest, at all that the company was besieged by what Ray called villains. The environment Mr. Lyre had created was the perfect breeding ground for an unhealthy workplace.

Gently, Vest asked, "So how does ENERGYMAN plan to defeat the villains at EPC?"

Ray sighed, then said, "I had been planning on giving my usual presentation to the company. The one where I describe the principles and concepts I learned working for you."

Vest nodded as Ray continued to speak.

While talking, Ray pulled a notepad and a pen out of his pocket and started to draw a familiar two-line chart that he used as a slide in most of his presentations.

"First, I ask people to *imagine* the ideal outcome, or *value*, that they want to create," Ray said, getting more excited, remembering how other workplaces had responded to his ideas.

PRINCIPLE: CONCEPT:

He kept writing as Vest looked on, smiling. He liked to see Ray feeling more positive about work.

Ray kept talking. "You have to be *involved* in the success of your career, the company, and your coworkers by feeling *empowered* and empowering others."

PRINCIPLE:

CONCEPT:

INVOLVE

EMPOWER

Ray thought about the examples he had given when he explained that point to different groups over the years. It seemed clear to him that *involvement* and *empowerment* were natural extensions of the *imagine the value you could create* concept, with which he would start his talk. He would ask people to think about the value they could imagine creating, specific to their own career: As the leader of their life, what did they want to create for themselves, their families, and their workplace? He would encourage people to come up with a basic, fact-based plan that only had to answer two questions: What would be the most effective thing to do in any situation? What would work? The value of looking at the facts versus the feelings of a situation often helped people see things clearly without feelings muddying the waters.

It was practice, Ray would explain, when he gave this presentation to a new group of workers. When someone felt agency—control—over their own success and goals, they felt stronger and more empowered. It was just like building any other skill or muscle. Small successes would help create a foundation of confidence that would support larger successes. And sometimes, most times, when colleagues were engaged and supportive of each other's successes, they created a pool of energy that further sustained and inspired each other. It was magic.

Ray wasn't a big fan of marketing speak, but the one phrase he did like was "virtuous circle." He imagined it in superhero terms—like a spinning sword or a glowing crown (or coin, he thought absently). A virtuous circle was a powerful force against the vicious cycle that would start when a workplace was infected with the opposite of good-faith thoughts and actions. When people were demotivated and fearful.

Empowerment, Ray knew, was the natural evolution from *involvement*. When people were able to be involved and to make positive changes, starting with themselves, they felt empowered. It gave them a glow, an energy that spurred them to keep achieving and stretching themselves. A common occurrence when that happened would be that other people would notice, become inspired, and start to push themselves to achieve more and be happy about doing so. Coworkers would gain strength and inspiration from each other's hard work and success. Ray had seen it time and time again—a single individual inspiring others would eventually reach a critical mass of involved and empowered employees. Very early on in the process of change, coworkers would start to positively reinforce and inspire each other to greater heights of success and positive impact.

It seemed that there was an interest and an appetite for positive change among many of the employees at EPC. They weren't bad people, but they were in a bad place.

Ray said to Vest, "And what better place to start a virtuous circle of energy than an energy-producing company?"

Vest pointed to the chart that Ray was drawing and asked, curiously, "What do you say to people when you're explaining how the principle of *informed* is connected to the concept of *keeping score*?

PRINCIPLE: CONCEPT:

INFORM

Score

Ray looked at where Vest was pointing and thought about how cool it was that he was explaining something back to Vest that Vest had taught him.

Ray started to reply, "I tell people that when I worked for you ..." Ray grinned at the memory, and Vest grinned back.

Ray continued, "I say that keeping score is an obvious way of knowing how the game is going. But when you are thinking about the game of life ..."

Ray slowed down as he thought about how he explained this concept: that life itself wasn't a game but that the principles of winning, or succeeding, were the same.

"That when you think of the end goal, of success, when the time frame is longer than a few hours, the only way to keep score, to keep track of where you are, is to stay *informed* of the progress."

Ray leaned back and stared at the field as he went deeper into the details of explaining the concept of keeping score to people who didn't automatically view work or life situations using the structure of a football game.

He said, "I try to explain that having information about your personal progress and staying informed about where you are in relation to your goals are what keeping score is all about. The biggest difference between using the principles you taught me and an actual football game is that no one has to lose in order for someone to win."

Ray paused, then said, "Well, I guess the villains lose. Each energy-sucking villain has a natural, positive counterpart."

Ray looked down at his chart and drew a list while he spoke.

"The counterpart to apathy is *interest*; chaos is *order*; procrastination is *action*; defeatism is a *winning mind-set*; fear is *confidence*; status quo is *change*; and negativity is *positivity*. All those words by themselves can't make people change. When people like the ones at EPC are stuck in an energy-depletion cloud, it really is a vicious cycle. They feel so discouraged and overwhelmed that they can't imagine a way out and they think that the problems are far too big to be fixed. So I like to remind them that every step forward is progress, and keeping track, or score, of each step allows them to see the consistent progress they are making. People need to know that no matter how small, each little bit of progress helps build a strong foundation on which they can build success."

Ray paused again and said, "Sometimes it is hard to see the progress, which is why I tell people it is crucial to keep score—to keep track and stay informed about everything they are doing that's part of the antivillain crusade. Anything that falls in the positive column counts and should be noted. If someone can look back and see how daily improvements build up, that gives them energy to keep going. And the only way to know what the score is, what the improving numbers look like, is to keep informed of the metrics that make up your every day."

Ray echoed another well-known business productivity saying: "What can be measured can be improved."

He looked down again at the chart that spelled out Vest's name.

Vest said, "So let me play this back to you."

Ray laughed. That was something Vest would say to him all of the time when they worked together.

Vest continued, "You have a demotivated and demoralized group of people. You ask them to trust you and imagine the value they could create for themselves, their careers, and the company. Then you empower them to make changes by giving them a lens into how they can positively make changes in the company. You get them more involved in the company's goals and the decisions so they not only feel but *know* that their actions can make a difference. Then you explain how staying informed of their progress is a form of keeping score of growth, change, and achievements."

Ray nodded. "Yes, that's absolutely right. I try to explain that the power of a 'vicious cycle' and 'virtuous circle' are exactly the same. The same way villains can spread like germs, so can heroes—positivity and energy. They are like opposite sides of a coin. If you just flip the coin to heads versus tails, then the actions people take can drive and create more energy and achievements."

Vest said, "Well, it's a good thing you have those Unbelievium coins working for you, then!"

Ray slowly said, "Yes. I think it is."

He hadn't told Vest that he had forgotten to bring the coins in with him or that he had rediscovered them on his desk. He knew Vest would understand and encourage him regardless of his forgetfulness.

PRINCIPLE:

CONCEPT:

INSPIRE

TRAIN

Vest looked down at the chart and asked, "So, how do you explain the final connection between the principle of *inspire* and the concept of *train*?"

Ray said, "I go back to a football game analogy. Even if someone doesn't know or play a sport, they certainly know that the only way to get better is to train themselves, whether that is to run more to increase endurance or practice throws to increase distance and accuracy."

Ray continued, "I encourage people to think back and share a time they worked at something bit by bit to get better. Maybe it was when they were a kid taking piano lessons or practicing yoga or lifting weights. I ask them to think back to how they started: first with the easy pieces or poses or lighter weights. Then, I ask if there was an end goal—did they ever say to themselves that when they could play a certain piece, do a certain pose, or lift a certain weight, they would stop? Pretty much everyone says no, that those were achievements that were markers on a path, not the end of the path. Then I asked them how they felt when the passed each mark—discovered by practicing every day that they were able to look back and see that things got easier and how they felt when they were able to lift a heavier weight amount or more easily hold a pose or play a piece that seemed complicated. Did they stop? Even the people who say they thought about stopping would then say they felt inspired to try the next thing. That's how I link the concept of training to inspiration. When you train yourself, practice keeping track of your progress by keeping score, and achieve goals on your path, you tend to feel inspired to do it again and again."

Ray looked up and smiled. "It really is a virtuous circle. It's all energy. When you invest in yourself, and your goals, you create energy that sustains you. The opposite side of that is what is happening at EPC now, where there is no investment in people or resources to empower them. That drains their energy. Energy builds energy—negative energy depletes and slows down a person and, by extension, their organization. With positive energy, the same process is in play, but it creates a positive ripple effect, creating energy and inspiring more production. And when people realize that they can create energy, they do."

Vest was smiling as he listened to Ray's voice become more energized and happier, describing how people and organizations could transform themselves into sustainable energy producers. He knew that Ray, with the Unbelievium coins on his side, would be able to convince people to listen to him and give his easy-to-understand chart a try.

But Vest was curious as to how Ray would do it.

Vest leaned forward and asked Ray, "How do you plan to get the folks at EPC on board, given how disempowered they feel right now?"

Ray looked down at his chart and wrote a line he heard Vest ask at the end of meetings they would have, back in the day. He answered as he wrote it down. "I'll just ask them, 'Are you all in?'"

Ray then said, "There are a few old employees, including John—the guy who built the model with Brian, the one Mr. Lyre sidelined—who are still there, and still remember how it was. They aren't the ones doing anything bad; they're just completely overworked and discouraged. It's a real testament to Brian's memory that they are even still there at all. I want to remind them of Brian and of the value that Brian imagined EPC would create. That's the starting point. I want them to imagine that that opportunity exists again. And if I can get them in that frame of mind, where they are imagining what EPC could be, rather than what it is today, I think that will put them in a space where they are open and excited and optimistic about change. And then I can go over this chart with them. Get their thoughts and ideas to sketch out a strategy to turn EPC around, to truly make it an energy-producing company both for our customers and our employees. I think if we have that conversation outside of the office and they feel empowered and excited and supported, it will stop the villains in their tracks and start to create a positive force in an upward direction. And if enough people start believing and acting in a positive way, I know, I just know, it will inspire others."

"That sounds like a good idea," said Vest.

Both men then settled back to watch the rest of the game.

But first, Ray sent out a quick email to a few employees who had made a good impression on him. He wrote that he knew it was last minute, but if they could make the time, he was inviting them over to a casual afternoon brainstorming session with pizza at his house tomorrow, Sunday evening.

Before the game ended with another win for the home team, everyone said they would be there.

Ray showed the positive responses to Vest, who tapped Ray on his shoulder.

"That's great!" Vest exclaimed. "You were right. There clearly is an appetite for change at EPC."

Ray agreed, and, feeling energized, he stopped by his local office-supply store and a nearby arts-and-crafts store for supplies. He had plans to make the impromptu Sunday gathering at his house as fun and engaging as possible for the EPC employees. He could feel their readiness and their hope for something good.

SUNDAY AFTERNOON

Ray sat in his den with seven other EPC employees. There was John, Brian's cocreator at EPC, as well as Polly, a call center employee who was famous for never losing her sense of humor or calm voice, no matter how upset the person on the other end of the phone was. In fact, against all odds, given EPC's dreadful customer service policies, Polly still managed to retain more customers and post the highest call center satisfaction rates every month. Sharon, the company's front desk receptionist, was the unofficial office manager. It was only unofficial because the position of office manager had been open for quite a while, yet Mr. Lyre had hired no one to fill it. In the meantime, Sharon quietly undertook the tasks a regular office manager would do, as well as going above and beyond to recognize and celebrate people when she could. Despite the lack of energy that pervaded EPC, Sharon's continuous efforts always brought a smile to the faces of people who were on the receiving end of her attention and kindness. Bill, the CFO, was the only other employee besides John and Ray who came from executive management, and the rest of the attendees were from the in-field and engineering teams.

"Thank you all so much for coming to my house on such short notice," Ray said. "I'm so happy you could all make it!"

Bill said, "Miss an afternoon at Chuck E. Cheese's with four kids under the age of seven? I was delighted to get your email. Feel free to make this a weekly thing!"

The rest of the group laughed and relaxed.

Ray laughed too. He made a mental note to send Bill and his wife a gift certificate for a dinner for two at a nice restaurant in town, which would include a note of thanks to Bill's wife for sparing him on such short notice.

Ray took a deep breath and began to talk about the opportunity he saw at EPC. He said, "Some of you may have looked at my website before I started at EPC."

Everyone in the room raised their hand to show they had.

Ray asked, "Did any of you see the comic strip?"

Only Jeff raised his hand, while everyone else looked slightly confused.

"It's okay!" Ray said, smiling. "I don't make it that obvious on the site. Jeff, do you mind telling everyone else what you remember about the comic strip?"

Jeff laughed. "I remember it well, because I was a big comic book fan growing up. You're the character named ENERGYMAN, right?"

"That's right!" Ray said, delighted that Jeff had remembered. "Did you happen to notice the Reaction Gang, the villains in the comic strip?"

Sharon asked innocently, "Was one of them named Sammy?"

Everyone in the room laughed, while Sharon covered her face and laughed too.

Jeff kept talking about the comic strip. He said, "I remember thinking, at the time, I was happy we were going to get a superhero to come to EPC. Because the last time I thought of someone as a hero, it was Brian."

The room was quiet while everyone remembered Brian and what EPC had been like when he was still there.

Ray said, "I'm honored that you thought of me with the same hope you had when you began working with Brian. He was a really great person, wasn't he?"

Everyone nodded in agreement.

Ray continued, "It is that feeling of hope that I believe still exists at EPC today. It just needs to be brought back out. ENERGYMAN is my alter ego. When companies ask me to come in, often they say that they want help energizing or reenergizing a team. People don't start out depleted of energy, right?"

Everyone in the room nodded.

Ray said, "When you all started at EPC, you were imagining the value the company would provide to its customers."

Bill said thoughtfully, "I imagined the value it would provide to the world. Brian and John's invention has the power to revolutionize energy production worldwide, making it easier to provide at lower costs. It's nothing short of amazing."

Ray smiled understandingly. He was delighted to see how easily the people in the room slipped back into talking about EPC in a positive way.

Ray stood up and started writing on a large piece of paper.

He said, "Energy is a force. It's power. Who has powers? In comic-book terms, the people with superpowers are villains and heroes."

Ray wrote as he spoke. "When we get sick, viruses and germs deplete our energy. We have to rest, eat well, and take medicine to get better. When thinking about a company instead of an individual, you can think of viruses and germs, but you can also think of the things that deplete and drain energy as *villains*."

"Villains," Ray said as he finished writing, "are the illnesses that exhaust an organization."

Ray stood in front of the list as the people in the room read it, nodding in sad familiarity.

- apathy
- chaos
- fear
- defeat
- negativity
- procrastination
- status quo

"I can see you're familiar with some of these," Ray said.

He wanted to move the team quickly on to the positive.

"What are the counterparts to each one of these?"

The people in the room quickly yelled them out, excited. Now the chart looked like this:

apathy	INTEREST
chaos	ORDER
fear	CONFIDENCE
defeat	WINNING MIND-SET
negativity	POSITIVITY
procrastination	ACTION
status quo	CHANGE

Ray said, "Today I'd like for all of us to talk, and I want to hear your thoughts on how, together, we can vanquish the villains at EPC and get its energy back."

Ray then asked, "How many of you in here go to football games?"

Almost everyone in the room raised their hand.

Ray held up a poster board with four pictures on it: three glowing coins, a copy of the email he had sent to the group, a picture of a scoreboard, and a snapshot of Vest's face on a poster from the movie *Rocky*.

Ray said, "Right now this probably looks like a confusing jumble of pictures."

The group of EPC workers in his living room looked at him attentively.

Ray explained, "Football coaches use poster boards like this one to rapidly communicate ideas and concepts to their teams during a game. The pictures have to be specific and meaningful to have impact. They are unique to each coach and each team, sometimes to each player."

Ray held the poster while he continued to speak. "I have a simple two-line chart that lays out the principles and concepts that I think are the most inspirational. But words alone may not be enough to inspire you, let alone encourage you to participate in taking action."

He slowed down, giving his words more weight. "I'd like to try to explain those principles and concepts using these images and hear what you think. If it makes sense to you, I'd like to hear your thoughts on how we might use something like this to reenergize EPC."

Everyone in the room sat up straighter, with their eyes on Ray.

Ray thought, They have so much hope! This is a great sign.

Ray pointed to the first image on the board, the three glowing coins.

He took a deep breath.

He hadn't decided until this moment what he was going to tell the group about the Unbelievium coins.

Ray said, "These are Unbelievium coins."

He paused.

"They actually exist," Ray said.

He stuck his hand in his pocket and drew out the three glowing coins. The people in the room leaned closer, and Ray handed them out for everyone to pass around and to look at more closely.

As the people in the room passed the coins around, holding them gently and looking at them intensely, Ray talked about Vest. He described Vest as his mentor and talked about how he began working with Vest, and he pointed at Vest's picture on the board. He explained how Vest had given the coins to him and asked him to bring the coins with him into the office every day. Ray confessed to the group that he hadn't done so—in fact, that he had entirely forgotten about the coins until a few days before, when he noticed them glowing on his desk.

As Bill handed the coins back to Ray, Ray held them and said, "I asked Vest about these coins yesterday. Vest said a few years back he had to imagine how to create value at a time when there was a lull in attendance and increasing competition for families' discretionary income. People were spending their money and time on going to movies or restaurants or trips. They weren't spending their money on going to football games. Kids especially were spending more and more time in the online world, playing multiplayer video games, instead of playing or going to real-life sport games."

Ray explained how this was a relatively new issue, that before the internet had taken hold, people didn't have many options other than work or sports for positive, nonreligious community experiences.

He told the EPC employees that Vest had no playbook to follow. That he had to imagine a solution.

Ray said, "Vest told me that when he thought about how he was going to create value in attending the university football games, he noticed that these three coins, sitting in a pile of coins on his desk, were glowing.

"Vest told me that he had never seen those coins before. Vest didn't quite believe that he had created them out of his imagination, though he had no other explanation, so he decided to call them Unbelievium coins."

Ray then went on to explain how Vest had given the coins to him.

Ray said, "I think he gave them to me to use at EPC for the same reason, to help us imagine ways that we can create value again at EPC. That's the starting point. Here's the chart that I use, and you can see how much Vest has influenced me."

Ray drew out the chart and highlighted the letters that spelled Vest's name.

Underneath he wrote:

Are you all in?!

Principle	Imagine	Involve	Inform	Inspire
Concept	**V**alue	**E**mpower	**S**core	**T**rain

Are You All In?

Ray said, "This is the starting point that we talked about earlier—to imagine the value EPC can create for others and for ourselves. Let me talk through the other principles and the concepts they illustrate with you and how they are connected with the pictures on this board."

Ray explained that the image of the email invitation symbolized *involvement* and *empowerment*. He pointed out that everyone in the room had responded and were present. Ray asked the team in his den how they felt about getting that email and being present. They all agreed they felt stronger and more positive.

Polly said, "I really do feel oddly empowered just sitting here and having this conversation. It makes me feel like EPC was in the beginning—with a bright, shiny, exciting future in front of us. Us as the company and us as individuals who were making a difference. I feel stronger and more excited imagining EPC being that way again."

Everyone in the room nodded or said, "Yes, me too!" in agreement.

Ray felt great. That was exactly the reaction he had been hoping for.

Pointing to the picture of a scoreboard, Ray continued. "Presumably the concept of keeping *score* is clear, but the principle—in this case—is not about putting people in a win-or-lose situation but a win-win situation. *Score* is the conceptualization of the principle of keeping *informed*. If you know what your performance metrics are—like, say, for Polly it would be a score of nine or higher on customer satisfaction rates—then she is constantly *informed* of how she is doing on a regular basis. And staying informed about the score lets you make real-time (or game-time) decisions to adjust your performance."

"Finally," Ray said, "we come to Vest." He pointed at Vest's face. "I could talk about this man for days. But for the purposes of getting Bill back home in time to help put his four kids to bed ..."

"Ray, could you speak more slowly, please," Bill asked seriously, to laughs from everyone in the room.

Ray laughed as well. He said, "The meaning of putting Vest's face on top of the Rocky poster is that to me, he underscores the principle of *inspiration* and the importance of *training* as a part of staying inspired. The way Vest inspired me to strive to be better and better at what I do was by training me in his image."

Ray hastened to say, "Vest himself would *never* put it that way. But I stand by it. He inspires people by teaching them how to succeed. He didn't teach so much by talking. He taught me, and countless others, by doing a remarkable job at making people feel good, making them feel loved. Watching Vest do that for people made me want to learn how to do the same thing. He rarely gave specific instructions. It was more like he had this overall goal of providing such supernaturally good service in every situation that people were always left feeling tremendously loved. In an office environment, it often can be as simple as just doing what works. What is most effective in the moment to getting the job done right and making others feel involved, inspired, and empowered."

Ray took a sip of water. "So much for inspiring by doing versus talking," he joked.

Then he looked at the line he had written below the chart.

"So now I have a question for everyone here," Ray said.

He put on his sports-arena voice. The one that was meant to be heard across a stadium.

"Are you all in?" Ray boomed.

The EPC employees leaped up and shouted back, "All in!" with one voice. Then they laughed and collapsed back down on their seats, talking excitedly and peppering Ray with questions about Vest, as well as the overall principles and concepts. Ray passed around poster boards, markers, and other arts-and-crafts materials for people to take home with them.

After the pizza was eaten and his colleagues were helping clean up, Ray noticed that the Unbelievium coins were shining more brightly than they ever had before. It almost hurt his eyes to look at them. As Ray walked different people to the door, he quietly handed one Unbelievium coin each to John, Polly, and Sharon. He asked each of them to bring the coins with them into the office starting the next day.

He knew they wouldn't forget.

SUNDAY NIGHT

Ray tidied up his den, feeling more energized than he had been in months. He turned off the lights and started to head up to bed. Then he stopped for a moment and looked at the poster board with its pictures of the Unbelievium coins, the email invitation, a scoreboard, and Vest's face on the Rocky poster. He had drawn those Unbelievium coins better than he realized, he thought.

In the dark room, the drawing of the coins had almost seemed to be glowing.

IMAGINE A WORLD OF GOOD

Looking for your ticket to Pay It Forward? Scan the QR code below to gain access to three motivational virtual cards. Choose your favorite card and send it to your friends, coworkers, family members, or anyone who could use some positivity in their day!

Share how you Pay It Forward and find other inspirational posts using #InvestInSuccess.

THINK

of how you would like to inspire someone or how someone has inspired you.

SEND

one of the following inspirational cards to someone—a friend, a family member, a teacher—and show them how much you care.

SHARE

your ideas or story on Twitter, Facebook, and/or Instagram.

QUARTER 3

CHAPTER 7

BELIEF

MONDAY MORNING

The next morning, Ray woke up early and headed into the office. When he walked in, he saw Sharon sitting at the front desk with a big smile on her face and her poster board hung up neatly behind her. On the poster board was a square full of meticulously drawn smiles, almost too many to count; a picture of a steaming cup of coffee and a delicious-looking doughnut; a bumper sticker that read "Let Me Know How I'm Doing" with the "1-800" number crossed out and Sharon's email and phone number added in; and finally, a picture of a smiling Brian Lyre. At the bottom of the poster board, Sharon had written in neat letters, "Are you all in?" She was wearing a button that read, "All In!" and there was a basket of identical buttons on her desk, next to a box of doughnuts and an urn full of fresh, delicious-smelling coffee. Ray stood smiling, while Sharon grinned at him.

"Okay," Ray said. "I think I get it. The smiles are how many smiles you can create in a day in the people who walk by your desk and in this office; that's *imagine* and *value*. The cup of coffee and the doughnut … how you involve yourself in making the office run smoothly and empower yourself and others to feel happy? Through caffeine and sugar? In sports that's called juicing, Sharon. It's frowned upon."

Sharon cracked up and said, "I stand by it. Have a doughnut!"

Ray laughed and took a doughnut.

He said, "Okay, I'll allow it. I like that you're keeping score of how you're doing by giving people ways to tell you—that's great."

Ray then said, softly, "I see you have Brian's face up there. He's your inspiration, right?"

Ray wasn't sure how Brian's face also inspired *training*, and he was eager to hear Sharon's explanation.

Sharon said, "He was and he still is. Many people don't know that Brian used to teach classes after hours about how the energy-producing accelerator model worked and about the economic and health benefits of making energy available to all communities. He made it understandable to everyone. After he died, I registered for an online class in energy policies and economics so I could keep learning about energy—how it is made and how making energy available to people all over the world can help make their lives safer and better."

Ray stood there quietly, thinking about what an amazing person Brian had been. Then something bright and shiny caught his eye.

Sharon was waving her Unbelievium coin at him.

She said, "I'm keeping this right next to my keyboard as I work, and I carry it with me whenever I have to leave my desk."

She paused and said, "I'm not sure what else I'm supposed to be doing with it."

Ray responded, "That's okay. I don't know either. All I know is that I was supposed to bring them into the office. And through you and Polly and John, I have. I guess we'll find out more in time."

Sharon nodded, looked back at her poster, and smiled. Then she asked, "Would you like a cup of coffee?"

As Ray poured himself a cup of coffee, Polly walked in, and the three of them grinned at each other. When Polly saw the basket of "All In!" buttons, she high-fived Sharon, said "All in!," and pinned a button to her shirt. She was also carrying a poster board with the words "Are You All In?" written at the bottom. Polly was in a rush to get to her desk, but before she left the front area, Ray managed to see one image on the board: a picture of Brian Lyre.

After taking an "All In!" button, Ray walked through the building to John's office. He had noticed that John was always at the building earlier and later than anyone else. Part of the reason John was there for so many hours was because Mr. Lyre had given him the work of three people. Ray had come in early specifically that morning to sit down with John to discuss how they could lighten his workload.

Ray noticed a poster board hanging on the wall of John's office and saw, without surprise, Brian's familiar face beaming from the corner. John was playing with something shiny on his desk. Ray assumed it was the third Unbelievium coin, until he got closer. It looked like a very expensive toy, a bunch of thin rods and boxes made out of the most precious metals in the world.

"What is that? It's gorgeous!" Ray said to John.

John looked up, startled.

"Oh, hi!" John said. "I didn't hear you come in. You've never seen this before?"

"No," Ray said. "Should I have?"

"I guess not," John said, a little sadly. "You know that energy-producing accelerator we built for this region, right?"

Ray nodded.

"Well," John said, holding up the glowing item for Ray to look at, "this is the model for a global version. A combined energy-producing and accelerating model. A few of these in strategically placed areas could power a whole country. Brian and I began working on this after we finished the regional model. That one strengthens preexisting energy grids. This one can be used as the foundation for energy in parts of the world where there isn't a consistent or reliable source. It could improve the lives of billions of people."

John nodded toward the poster board on his wall. The model in Ray's hands was the picture in the *imagine/value* corner of the poster board, diagonally across from Brian's picture.

"It's beautiful," Ray said. "Will you explain to me how it works?"

John looked up, excited. "Sure!" he exclaimed.

"But first you need to understand how the regional model works—or would have worked—had we actually produced it."

Ray sat down and listened to John speak in clear, concise sentences. Ray asked a few questions about the cost and deployment of the original regional model. John explained, in detail, how the energy-producing accelerator would have strengthened the local electricity grid, expanding its reach and strength to neighboring grids, while at the same time lowering costs for customers. Then John explained how the global model would work. He explained how billions of people currently living in areas with no energy would benefit from having a reliable source.

Ray's head was spinning. The value of consistent energy included improved living conditions, access to education, transport, water, fresh food, health care, and opportunity for the entire world.

How on earth, he wondered, was EPC not the most well-known and successful company on the planet, with an invention like this as an asset?

Ray, dazed with the possibility, thanked John for explaining the potential positive impact of EPC's energy models and got up to go to his office.

"Ray, wait!" John said behind him.

Ray turned back inquiringly.

John held up his Unbelievium coin. It was shining brightly.

"I didn't forget!" John said.

"Thank you, John," Ray said.

He was touched. Sharon, Polly, and John all brought the Unbelievium coins in with them the day after they were asked to do so. Ray, on the other hand, hadn't remembered when his dearest friend and mentor had asked him. He wondered what lesson there was in that for him as he walked toward Bill's office, in the financial department.

Ray spent half an hour with Bill, during which he explained that he was authorizing immediate availability of funds for John to restart and launch the local EPC project. Bill leaned back in his chair, under a newly installed poster board. Ray wasn't surprised to see Brian's face on it. Bill had joined EPC only a week before Brian's death, but the two men had gone to college together.

Bill said, "You know, Mr. Lyre has told me that only he has the power to authorize any expense over fifty thousand dollars."

Ray just looked at Bill, who was smiling.

"But as CFO," Bill continued, "I have a fiduciary responsibility to the shareholders of the company and the board to release funds that will have a positive, measurable impact for the company. The funds will be available by noon. I'll let John know he can send me any contracts he needs cosigned and that I'll work with legal to get them back to him as soon as possible."

Ray was pleased. He hoped his next question wouldn't put Bill over the edge.

"Could you also free up the funds for a company-wide pizza party on Friday?" he asked.

Bill grinned. "It would be my pleasure," he replied.

Throughout the rest of the morning, Ray managed to walk by the desks and offices of everyone who had been at his house the night before. Each one of them had a newly designed poster board hanging by their desk. In a few cases, he noticed them explaining the meaning of the board to one or more colleagues. When Ray walked by Polly's desk in EPC's call center, he noticed a crowd of people by her desk, listening and taking notes.

Ray got to his office and sent off an email to Mr. Lyre, carbon-copying the board of directors and Bill, informing them of the new funds he directed Bill to make available to John, effective immediately. He added he was looking forward to hosting his first company town hall as president on Friday and invited all the board members to attend.

Then Ray sent a note to the employees who had been at his house the night before. He thanked them again for coming and for taking his poster board example to heart. In the email Ray wrote that he noticed people had been asking questions about the poster boards. He ended the email by asking them to tell their colleagues that if they wanted to create poster boards of their own, there were ample supplies in the cafeteria area for them to use.

That day went by in a flash. While Ray hadn't mentioned anything to anyone in the office other than John or Bill (and Mr. Lyre) about the new funding for the regional model deployment, it seemed everyone in the office had heard about it by lunch. Ray himself had a rare lunch out of the office with a few members of the board for a previously scheduled check-in to see how he was settling in at EPC. Mr. Lyre had been invited to the lunch but declined to attend, citing a previous engagement. Mr. Lyre was disinclined to attend any meeting with board members that didn't include those who were his close personal friends.

MONDAY AFTERNOON

When Ray returned from lunch, he noticed Sharon was looking thoughtful and more subdued than she had been early in the morning.

Ray asked, "What are you thinking about, Sharon?"

Sharon looked at Ray thoughtfully and said, "You know how Mr. Lyre always leaves for lunch at noon and never comes back into the office afterward?"

Ray nodded. He knew.

Sharon continued, "Well, today, when he came into the office at nine a.m., I saw him look at Brian's picture on the poster board behind my desk. He didn't say anything, and I remember thinking that I hoped seeing it didn't upset him."

Ray had wondered about that himself after seeing Brian's face in unexpected places around the office. He felt bad for not thinking earlier about how that might make Mr. Lyre feel.

Sharon continued, "But then, guess what? Mr. Lyre came back into the office just a few minutes before you did. He didn't say anything, but when he walked by my desk, he took a doughnut, and he smiled!"

Sharon took a moment, considering. "Of course, he was smiling at the doughnut, not me, but still … it was a smile. I don't think I've ever seen him smile before."

Ray was shocked, then delighted. He high-fived Sharon and went to his office, where there was another Mr. Lyre–related shock awaiting him. It was a response to Ray's email about the funds he had directed Bill to make available to John, and the first email response

Mr. Lyre had ever sent to Ray. The board was still carbon-copied on the email, ensuring they all would see it.

Mr. Lyre's email consisted of only four words: "Okay. Good idea. Thanks."

Ray sat back in his chair, stunned.

He never thought he would get an email from Mr. Lyre, let alone one consisting of a compliment and a thank-you.

CHAPTER 8
SAME HERE

MONDAY AFTERNOON

Ray was sitting in his office, processing the unexpected email from Mr. Lyre, when his email alert sound chimed. There were two new emails in his inbox—one from Polly, one from John—and both said the same thing: "I need to talk to you right away. Are you free?"

Ray responded immediately to both emails, writing that Polly and John should feel free to come by his office.

John and Polly arrived at the same time, both breathing heavily. Clearly, they had run there.

"What's going on, guys?" Ray said, concerned.

Polly and John looked at each other. John gestured at Polly to go first.

Polly said, "Ray, a few people came up to my desk this morning, asking about the poster board, and I told them about what you told us and what the images on my board meant to me, and that if they were interested, there were supplies in the cafeteria."

"Same here," John said.

"But," Polly continued, "I didn't say anything about the Unbelievium coins. I'm not sure why."

"Same," said John.

"Okay," said Ray. He was still confused as to why they both needed to see him so urgently.

Polly looked at John. "Did something weird happen with your coin?" she asked.

"Yes!" yelled John. He gave a huge sigh of relief. "I thought I was going nuts!"

"What? What happened?!" asked Ray.

"Well," Polly said, "when I went out to lunch, I locked the desk drawer where I keep confidential records, petty cash, and the Unbelievium coin. When I came back, instead of just the one Unbelievium coin, there were *forty-five!*"

John jumped up from his seat. "Same for me!" he cried. "I put my Unbelievium coin in my pocket, and when I came back from lunch, there were twenty-five coins neatly lined up in front of my keyboard. And I keep my office door locked because of the proprietary nature of the files on my computer and in my desk. Legal insists on it."

The three of them looked at each other.

Ray said, "Polly, how many people asked you about your poster board today?"

Polly said, "I wasn't really keeping track. At first it was just one or two people, but then it became a few groups of people at different times. And then I saw some people talking to other people, so I guess all told, the entire department knows about the meaning behind the board now, what the principles and the concepts are."

Understanding dawned on Polly's face. She said, "And there are forty-five other people in the department!"

John added, "I know that all twenty-five people in my department know about the poster board, because we had our team meeting outside of my office today. One person asked about it, and I explained the board's principles and concepts to everyone then. I was glad you sent the email out about the supplies available for people to make their own boards, because I was able to tell everyone about that before lunch. I saw a bunch of people heading that way with pictures printed out."

Ray said, "Well, I guess I don't have to tell you two what to do now."

Polly and John looked at each other and laughed as they stood up.

Polly said, "Nope!"

John grinning, said, "I got it."

They each went back to their desks, gathered up the Unbelievium coins, and spent the rest of the day giving each member of their teams an Unbelievium coin and an explanation. About half of their coworkers already had poster boards hung up at their desks, while the other half were busy designing their own.

During the rest of the week, people throughout the company asked about the poster boards. Whomever they asked would subsequently find extra Unbelievium coins to give to them.

By the end of the week, practically every person in the company had a poster board with four images hanging behind their desk. People were more engaged with each other than ever before. They walked from desk to desk, learning what the different pictures on each board meant to each person and why those pictures were chosen. They talked about what value they imagined creating, how they felt more involved in EPC's mission and their own jobs, and how they were empowered to make a difference as a result. People in the same department shared ideas about how they kept score of their achievements and progress, exchanging ideas about the metrics and the type of tracking they were using. And a new company catchphrase became ubiquitous overnight. People would end meetings with the question, "Are you all in?" And everyone present would respond, loudly and cheerfully, "All in!" It became common to hear the "All in!" cry at various points throughout the day. And it never failed to make Ray smile.

On every poster board across the company, Brian's face shone from the corner marked *inspire/train*. John had found videos of the classes Brian taught about how the energy model worked and the economic benefits of inexpensive energy availability. He posted the talks on the company intranet and told Ray that they had been accessed and downloaded company-wide. He added that people wanted to learn about the global model, so he had spent a night recording a new class to explain how that worked. People were so interested that he created tests for people to take and score so they could see how much they were learning. He noted that so many people asked if the classes would restart that he agreed to teach one directly after the company-wide meeting on Friday.

Ray was delighted to hear it and promptly signed up to take the class himself.

There was a new feeling in the air at EPC. The company seemed invigorated and energized.

A few people had reported seeing Mr. Lyre walking around the company, looking at the poster boards, and smiling.

CHAPTER 9
VIRTUOUS CIRCLE

FRIDAY MORNING

It was Friday morning, and almost everyone in the company had an Unbelievium coin of their own and knew about how they multiplied when asked about. The energy in the air felt transformative. People were coming into work early, staying late, and vying with each other to share new ideas about how they were doing better (and feeling better) at their jobs. And everyone was excited for the upcoming town hall meeting and pizza lunch on Friday.

When Ray entered the office on Friday morning, Sharon had a doughnut and coffee waiting for him, along with a question.

She said, "You know how every time someone asked about the poster board, the person asked would find an Unbelievium coin or coins to give to the person who asked?"

Ray nodded.

Sharon continued, "Well, other than you, no one ever actually asked me about my poster board. People learned about them mostly from their department manager or the people they sit next to. But this morning, when I came into the office, I found two additional Unbelievium coins in my desk drawer."

She paused, then said, "I think I'm supposed to give one to you. And the other … to Mr. Lyre. Do you think that would be okay?"

Ray said, "I'd be honored to have one back, as long as that means you're keeping one for yourself. And I think that giving one to Mr. Lyre would be a very kind gesture."

Sharon said, "I'm so glad you agree! I wrote him a note. I wanted him to hear from me why Brian's face was on my poster board, what it meant, and how the Unbelievium coins have worked. I know he's been really difficult as a manager, but I have to think he couldn't have been that bad as a father if Brian was as amazing as he was, you know?"

Ray nodded, slowly. He hadn't thought of that before.

Sharon added, "Since you have to walk by his office on the way to yours, would you mind dropping it off for me? I can't leave my desk until lunch, and Sammy hasn't been in since Monday."

Ray took the card for Mr. Lyre from Sharon and asked, "Sammy hasn't been in? Do we know if he's okay?"

Sharon shrugged. "I don't know. All I know is that Mr. Lyre felt obligated to hire him because he's the nephew of one of the board members. He's never been able to hold down a job. He never added anything positive to this office anyway. All he did was gossip."

Ray thanked Sharon for the doughnut and coffee and walked over to Mr. Lyre's office, where, for the first time ever, the door was wide open. Bill was sitting inside the office, at the conference table, with a pile of paper in front of him.

"Ray," Mr. Lyre said, without inflection. "Come on in. There's something I wanted to discuss with you. Would you mind closing the door, please?"

As Ray turned around to close the office door, he noticed a poster board on the table in Mr. Lyre's office. In each of the four corners was a neatly affixed picture of Brian.

QUARTER 4

CHAPTER 10
ENERGIZED

FRIDAY AT NOON: EPC TOWN HALL MEETING AND PIZZA LUNCH

After a few hours, Ray left Mr. Lyre's office. Bill had left a few minutes before, giving Ray time to hand Sharon's note and Unbelievium coin to Mr. Lyre, who took them with thanks.

It was almost noon when Ray walked to the cafeteria, and the hum of the happy employees filled the air. As everyone in the company settled in their seats with their pizza, Ray walked up to the front of the room. He said that he would start the meeting with a few questions.

"I've noticed the poster boards by everyone's desks and the buttons a lot of you are wearing," Ray said. "I thought you might want to hear about how these poster boards and buttons are having a real impact, beyond each one of us individually."

Ray had previously gotten permission to call on a few people beforehand. He wanted to make sure everyone was comfortable sharing what an image, principle, and concept meant to them.

"First," Ray said, "When I say *imagine*, what concept comes to mind?"

"Value!" yelled back the company.

"Bill," Ray shouted. "Do you mind sharing what image you have on your board for *imagine and value?*"

"Not at all," Bill said, smiling broadly. "It's a mock-up of the EPC share price at one thousand dollars a share."

People applauded, whistled, and cheered.

"Okay," said Ray. "Next question. What do you all think about when I say *involve?*"

"*Empower*," came from everyone in the room.

There were more cheers. The company cafeteria was starting to sound more like a sports stadium on game night than an office conference room.

Ray said, "Okay, I picked someone on the crisis repair team to answer this question." He continued, "Because they are responsible for *empowering* people in this region."

The entire room groaned at Ray's pun.

Jeremy, a young man who trained as an electrician before joining EPC, stood up shyly. He had agreed to Ray's request, but he was still nervous about speaking in front of crowds.

"Well," Jeremy said, "I put a picture of a text bubble and EM-PWR (36-797). We posted about this text option online, and now people in the community can immediately text as well as call in or email us when they notice an energy issue. That way we can track issues in real time through community involvement, without energy outages having to reach critical mass like they usually do before a company finds out about it. And it's worked really well so far! People understand it is just to report an issue, and they seem to appreciate the ease of texting the information rather than using their phone's battery power to make a call."

The room clapped and cheered. This was a great idea! People were eager to conserve mobile phone batteries during a power outage, and long hold times to report an issue provoked anxiety. Everyone was delighted with the simple text solution.

Ray then gestured to Polly, who jumped up and ran to the front of the room.

"Hi!" she said.

"Hi!" the people in the room yelled back.

Polly said, "Working in the call center, we get scored all the time, in real time, based on how many people hang up angry or happy, get what they want, or change their mind about canceling their account. But until Ray explained his principles and concepts, I didn't understand that keeping score wasn't a matter of winning or losing points but instead about keeping myself informed about how I was doing at my job. And I knew I wasn't the only one who wanted to figure out ways to do my job better by keeping customers happier. After work on Tuesday, the entire call center agreed to stay around for an extra hour and brainstorm ways to solve customer problems or concerns and how to score ourselves on how we were doing."

Polly continued, "We came up with a lot of great ideas, and we're trying them out in different groups to see how they do. But one that we all decided to use right away was the donating discount program to measure customer retention."

About half the people in the room nodded while the other half looked mystified.

Polly said, "I know not everyone knows what that is, so I'll explain briefly. Electric bills are often rounded up or down to the full cent when a customer ends the month on an amount that is smaller than one quarter or three quarters of a cent. So if you end up with a bill that ends in $0.025 or $0.075, we'll round the first one down to the nearest dollar and the second one up to the nearest dollar."

Polly took a deep breath and continued, "Brian had started a donation discount option, where people could choose to round up their electric bill to the nearest cent or dollar and donate that amount back to the grid for use in less well-off neighborhoods or when disasters occur. We've been offering this program to people who dial in with issues or who want to cancel, and, so far, one hundred percent of people we offer it to choose it. What's more, Linda had the idea to try to use this to get old customers who left us back, so we've been emailing and calling people proactively, letting them know this is an option if they'd be interested."

Polly smiled hugely. "We have an unheard-of ninety percent positive response rate, and every single one of the people who have come back to us has *also* referred new customers to us, based solely on this program! They are telling their friends, their neighbors, even their workplaces to look into EPC for their energy needs, purely based on this donation discount program. In just this last week, our customer satisfaction and retention rate scores are through the roof. The response tracking shows us the types of things our customers are interested in and that make them happier."

Polly paused, overjoyed but not sure what to say next. She concluded, "It's just tremendous!"

The room clapped and cheered louder than ever.

Finally, Ray called John up to the front of the room and asked him to talk about the final corner of the board: the inspire and train corner.

John said, "I know for me the inspire/train corner of my poster board is a picture of Brian's face. And I think I'm not alone in that."

People started clapping, and some started crying. The applause didn't stop for a long time.

John said, "What people may not know is that Brian helped me train myself to think outside of the box, quite literally. Energy producers tend to run boxes, transformer boxes, and the model that we designed allowed us to think outside of that type of box. It let us strengthen the grid by spreading out the demand beyond just the physical boxes. It's pretty revolutionary, and it wouldn't have happened if we hadn't constantly trained ourselves to think outside what was possible, which really goes back to the first principle/concept pair Ray taught me of 'imagine/value.' We—Brian and I—imagined something that couldn't be done, that hadn't been done before, and that would create value for all whom it benefited: customers, business partners, employees, and shareholders. And I'm proud to say that we're back on track to that mission."

John started to head off the stage but had to double back to reassure people that the training session about energy creation was still on for after the pizza meeting. Everyone in the room was planning on attending.

The company applauded again as John made his way back to his seat. Everyone looked at Ray, expecting him to get back up to continue the meeting. Ray just sat there, smiling, as the EPC employees looked around, confused. Surely the meeting wasn't over yet?

Then Mr. Lyre walked up to the front of the room and stood there, looking out at the crowded space. It was quiet.

He said, "I am very proud of my son, Brian. I am proud of what he created here, in all of you. I did not understand it, and I am not proud of that. However, I am proud to see what an inspiration he was and continues to be to all of you, in ways I am still learning about, even today."

Mr. Lyre looked over the crowd and found Sharon. He winked, and Sharon winked back. Mr. Lyre continued, "To honor Brian's memory and continue his inspiration, Bill and Ray joined me in my office this morning, signing documents that give each person in this room one thousand block shares of stock, effective immediately."

Mr. Lyre held up his hand as people started cheering. "There's more," he said.

"I signed one more piece of paper today. It was my resignation letter," Mr. Lyre said.

The room was silent.

"My son and John built a great company that they knew how to manage well. I can best honor their achievements by finding the best people to manage EPC. However, I will still be at the ceremony tomorrow morning, when we flip the switch on the new Energy-Producing Company accelerator."

Mr. Lyre put his hand in his pocket and pulled out one of Sharon's buttons. As he pinned it to his suit, he said, "I am all in."

Ray stood up, clapping and cheering, and the rest of the company joined him.

As Ray walked to the front of the room, where Mr. Lyre was still standing, the two men shook hands. Then Ray said into the microphone, "I hope you'll all agree that Mr. Lyre shouldn't just be at the ceremony—he should be the one to flip the switch on the new model." Ray added, "Are you all in?"

As one, everyone in the room shouted back at top volume, "All in!"

The applause was deafening and didn't stop for nearly ten minutes. Every person in the company stood in line to shake Mr. Lyre's hand, to share their memories of Brian, and to thank him.

After each employee shook Mr. Lyre's hand, he gave them a small envelope. Each contained a gift card with a log-in and password for access to twenty prepaid classes at any online curriculum to be taken in any area they wished. They could take management courses, technology courses, business classes, energy classes, certification courses, or continuing education courses. Each gift card was in honor of Brian, in recognition of his inspiration and the importance of training, of continuing to learn, as part of staying continually inspired. The note also contained Mr. Lyre's private email address and read that he would be happy to personally underwrite any continuing education people at EPC wished to explore, also in memory of his son, Brian.

Ray hadn't known about this part of Mr. Lyre's plan and was touched anew. He couldn't wait to see Vest on Saturday and tell him all about everything incredible that had happened at EPC over the last week, thanks in great part to the miraculous, supernatural, unbelievable Unbelievium coins.

CHAPTER 11
SPOTLIGHT

SATURDAY MORNING: PRESS CONFERENCE

On Saturday morning the EPC press conference went off without a hitch. The interest in the EPC accelerator was beyond what anyone expected. Other energy companies across the country and the world were interested in buying patented equipment from EPC. Analysts on TV and in the press predicted that the EPC stock price would soar when the market opened on Monday and that the company would be able to use its new funds to invest more deeply into research, development, and the manufacturing of its global energy device, as well as hiring new employees and building additional offices worldwide.

By the time the press conference brunch ended, Ray had just enough time to drive to the stadium without breaking the speed limit. Unusually, on this Saturday, it was both the last game of the season and homecoming; that meant it was going to be a huge day at the stadium. The day before, on Friday afternoon, Ray's new assistant, Stuart Sanguine, had given him an envelope, hand delivered by a courier service. The envelope was from Vest and contained an admittance ticket to a special seating area for the last game of the season.

Vest had written on the envelope, "Don't be late!"

SATURDAY AFTERNOON

As Ray drove to the game, he thought about how much had changed since the first game of the football season. He couldn't believe that he ever considered turning down the job at EPC, nor could he have imagined how happy being at EPC made him. After Ray parked his convertible, he checked his suit jacket pockets. He had the envelope from Vest in one pocket. In his other pocket, there was an envelope that had been handed to him right before the press conference earlier that morning. He had only had the time to read it over once since then.

Ray locked his car and ran up the steps to the path into the stadium. There were three Unbelievium coins in his pocket again. When Ray got home on Friday night, he had discovered two more Unbelievium coins waiting on his side table, next to the front door. Together with the one Sharon gave him, they rested in his pocket, where they didn't jingle but chimed gently as he jogged down the path to the stadium.

When he reached the main stadium entrance, Ray stopped short.

He saw that the patch of grass planted at the start of the season had grown in.

The new statue was in place. It was a statue of Vest. There was a spotlight shining on Vest's smiling face, a smile so familiar and so beloved by so many.

Ray swallowed against a huge lump in his throat.

Ray then realized what the special admittance seating was for: to hear the president of the university officially honor Vest with the statue. As Ray hurried into the stadium, he saw that he wasn't the only person smiling with tears in his eyes. He took his seat on the platform with the honoree, giving him a high five as he sat down beside Vest.

CHAPTER 12

HERO

SATURDAY AFTERNOON: HOMECOMING, LAST GAME OF THE SEASON

Less than five minutes later, the president of the university began to speak. He spoke about the many contributions Vest made not only to the stadium but to the students that Vest made a point of hiring to work at the stadium. He spoke of how much those jobs meant to those students then, and how so many of them had since credited their subsequent career success to working for Vest. The president then mentioned how the university enjoyed a higher-than-average percentage of students who contributed to the scholarship fund and how many of them did so in honor of Vest.

The president continued to speak about how Vest inspired confidence and success in all of those who worked at the stadium, played at the stadium, and came to the stadium to have a good time. Then he noted that the combination of the homecoming game and final game of the season meant that this game was the one traditionally attended by the most alumni.

"To that end," said the president of the university, "there is no better game at which to announce that we are starting a new scholarship fund in Vest's name and honor, in addition to the statue in front. Thank you, Vest."

Ray began to cry tears of joy as he stood, along with the rest of the stadium, to cheer Vest. As a former scholarship student himself, he knew how critical scholarship funding was and how it changed so many lives for the better.

The university president raised his hands to say something else. People quieted down but remained standing.

"Our goal," the university president said, "is to run the largest and most transparent scholarship fund in the nation, used solely for student support. If all you alumni and everyone else present would kindly now check under your seats, you'll find an envelope where you can include a check or a commitment to the Vest Scholarship Fund."

The crowd roared without stopping as a blizzard of white envelopes began to cover the field.

Ray took the second envelope from his pocket, the one handed to him by the chairman of the EPC board of directors. It contained a $1 million check, a bonus for turning EPC into the powerhouse it was always meant to be. Ray turned the check over, endorsed it, and wrote, "Donated in full to the Vest Scholarship Fund" on it. Then he nudged Vest and handed it to him. Vest glanced at it and smiled more widely than Ray had ever seen him do before.

It was an exciting game that went on far longer than usual. By the time the stadium emptied out and Ray and Vest were on their way to the homecoming reception, it was full dark.

Ray, hoarse from all the cheering, had one more thing he wanted to say to Vest. It was about the Unbelievium coins.

"I paid them all forward," Ray told Vest. "They multiplied, and then the original three came back to me. And now I think I'm supposed to give them back to you."

Ray reached into his pocket to hand the coins back to Vest, but every time he tried to hand them over, they wouldn't go.

Vest laughed.

"Ray," he said. "Those coins will stay with you until you find another person who needs as much help as you did when you told me you wanted to quit EPC before you had even started."

Vest paused.

"Do you remember what I said to you, all those years ago, when you came to find me, right after you heard you got into the university on a scholarship?"

Ray looked back at Vest, remembering that day and the cold, rainy night before it. More than twenty years ago, a lost young man felt more alone than he had ever felt before. The man in front of him had saved him that night.

"You said, 'Pay it forward,'" Ray said, his voice thick with emotion.

"I have, Vest," Ray promised. "And I will."

Vest said, "Are you all in?"

Ray flipped over his jacket collar, showing Vest the button he had been wearing all day.

He grasped Vest's hand.

Ray said, "All in."

THE
END

INVEST!

Key Takeaways

INVEST!

KEY TAKEAWAYS

The following lessons are the key takeaways from *INVEST!*

Imagine

- Create value by suspending disbelief and determining a brighter future.

- Identify great leadership.

- Determine the direction by communicating a compelling vision based on shared values.

- Show them the way by developing clear SMART goals that align with the vision.

Involve

- Empower people to make decisions that provide supernatural service.

- Ask everyone to contribute and connect everyone to the mission.

- Take actions that are aligned with shared values.

Inform

- Keep score by measuring what's important.

- Grow your genius.

- Hold everyone accountable for performance by creating key performance indicators.

Inspire

- Provide opportunities for continuous improvement through training.

- Fall in love with what you do and show people that you care.

- Reward innovation and the behaviors you'd like to see.

INVEST!

Study Guide

INVEST! QUESTIONS FOR REVIEW

Q1

Chapter 1 -What personal dilemma does Ray face?

-What is Ray's comfort zone?

-What is Ray's talent?

-Why is the stadium a "happy place"?

-Why is Vest called a Rock Star?

-What leadership principles did Ray learn?

-Describe the perfect day.

Chapter 2 -What made Energy Production Company (EPC) successful? What caused the downfall?

-What is the value proposition of EPC?

-What is Ray's leadership doctrine?

-What is Mr. Lyre's leadership style?

-How has it affected the company?

-What role does trust play?

Chapter 3 -What is the significance of the coins?

-Why did Vest give the coins to Ray?

Q2

Chapter 4 -What did Vest say to Ray to get him to consider taking the job?

-What did Ray originally believe about workers?

-What did he learn?

-How successful has Ray been in past ventures? How do we know?

-What was Ray most proud of from previous job engagements?
-What is the "Jesus Ticket" concept?
-Why is it important for employees to be shareholders?
-How would Ray run EPC if he were in charge?

Chapter 5 -Why does EPC need a new kind of leader?
-What are the challenges faced by EPC? What are the immediate challenges faced by Ray in his effort to turn around the company? What future challenges will he face?
-What are the trends in EPC's bottom line?
-What response did Ray receive when he discussed the company's declining performance with Mr. Lyre?
-What did Ray learn about the company after he joined?
-Why is Mr. Lyre resistant to the idea of implementing the energy accelerator?
-What is Ray's opposing point of view?

Chapter 6 -Why is it important to "fall in love with what you do"?
-What is "supernatural service"?
-What does it mean to "grow your genius"?
-Why was it important for Ray to take the coins with him every day?
-Who are the Reaction Gang? What role do they play?

-Describe the vicious cycle at the company. What is the effect of the vicious cycle on the company?

-What leadership concepts did Ray learn from Vest?
-How are the concepts related to leadership principles?
-How do these concepts apply to EPC?

Q3

Chapter 7   -What does it mean to be "All In"? Why is it important?
-How do the leaders keep hope alive? Why is this important?
-What is special about the company's history?
-What are the positive attributes of John's idea, the energy accelerator?
-How are employees empowered?

Chapter 8   -What is the purpose of the poster boards?
-How do Polly and John initially react to the poster boards and the coins? What happened after lunch?
-What was the impact of the poster boards and coins? Why?

Chapter 9   -What caused the coins to multiply?
-Describe the virtuous circle at the company. Why is it important? How does it work?
-What have the company's past hiring and appointment decisions been based upon? Why?

Q4

Chapter 10 -How was value created for the company?

-How were employees empowered?

-How did Jeremy and Polly keep score?

-Why did employees of the call center hold a brainstorming session? What were the results?

-What affect did training have on John? What opportunities were available for employees?

-What change occurred in Mr. Lyre? Why did this change occur?

-What was the significance of the "All In" button?

-How were employees energized?

Chapter 11 -How did energized employees affect the bottom line of the company?

-What was the significance of the statue?

Chapter 12 -How did the university benefit from Vest's service?

-How will it benefit in the future?

-How has life come full circle for Ray?

-How did the university's investment in Ray payoff?

-Why wouldn't the coins go back to Vest?

-How did Ray pay it forward?

INVEST!

FINAL QUESTIONS FOR REFLECTION

The following questions may be used to stimulate lively discussions about *INVEST!*

1. What is the key to the success of the company?

2. Are the problems solvable? If so, how?

3. What is the resistance to solving the problems?

4. What were the most important contributions of Vest, Ray, and Brian?

5. If given the opportunity to start over, should Ray do anything differently? If so, what specifically?

6. What strategies can be used to effectively communicate the vision/mission of an organization?

7. What are the keys to creating a culture of accountability?

8. What are the benefits to providing employees with training and development opportunities?

9. What are the best ways to recognize employee performance?

10. What are the keys to creating an entrepreneurial and innovative workplace?

THE **REACTION GANG**

APATHY

CHAOS

FEAR

DEFEAT

PROCRASTINATION

STATUS QUO

NEGATIVITY

ABOUT THE AUTHOR

Dr. Mumford, professor of sport management and founding executive director of the Center for Global Sport Leadership at Central Michigan University, is a thought leader, a change agent, and a foremost authority on leadership and building high performance work teams. He speaks at conferences around the world. He taught leadership for the Disney Institute at Walt Disney World in Orlando, Florida. He was recognized by the American Red Cross as a Michigan Hero and by the United Nations for his humanitarian efforts.

Dr. Mumford is a graduate of the Institute for Management and Leadership in Education at Harvard University. He has received many honors and awards, including the United States Marine Corps Commander's Award, the Volunteers Are Central Award, and the Michigan Campus Compact Community Service Learning Award; he was also named a Holmes Scholar and Outstanding Mentor of the Year.

He has been appointed to numerous committees and advisory boards, including with the United Way, the YMCA, *Athletic Management*, the Angel Wings Fund, and the National Football League (NFL). He is frequently called upon to consult or speak on various subjects, such as leadership, change, marketing, fundraising, and strategic planning.

His mission is to create ideas, products, and brands that inspire dreams.

For more information, please visit:

www.VINCEMUMFORD.com.

9 781642 251364